AMIA: AN ONGOING CRIME

EXTENDED EDITION

ALBERTO L. ZUPPI

Copyright © 2018 by Alberto L. Zuppi

All rights reserved.

No part of this book may be reproduced in any form or by any electronic or mechanical means, including information storage and retrieval systems, without written permission from the author, except for the use of brief quotations in a book review.

ISBN 978-1-949864-10-6

*Dedicated to the victims and the families of the victims of the AMIA bombing,
and for persevering on their search for justice.*

CONTENTS

1. July 18th, 1994, 9:53 A.M.	1
2. Corruption	9
3. Nazis In Argentina	19
4. Memoria Activa	33
5. The Tape	45
6. Reading	59
7. Collateral Damage	73
8. The Final Drop	93
9. Going International	103
10. On Trial	125
11. Revolution	145
12. The Judgment	159
Epilogue	169
Afterword	183
Acknowledgments	185
About the Author	187

1

JULY 18TH, 1994, 9:53 A.M.

The battery was dead, the heater useless; the policemen seated in the patrol car outside 633 Pasteur Street were freezing. Another officer had already taken the dead battery to be recharged, leaving the car's hood slightly open, and they awaited his return. Bordón sat reading the sports section of the newspaper—just yesterday, Brazil had won the Soccer World Cup—while Sergeant Guzman, in the driver's seat, watched the street. A truck had parked, and, in the process of removing a filled dumpster from the curb, blocked the lane. Waiting then for the truck to deposit a new, empty dumpster, the motorists to its rear had made their impatience known. When the driver had finally finished the task and departed, the morning traffic began to pour past again, emptying onto Avenida Córdoba two blocks away.

Guzman returned his gaze to the building at 633 Pasteur, where a group of Jewish philanthropic institutions had organized the *Asociación Mutual Israelita Argentina*. Ever since the bombing of the Israeli Embassy in 1992, organizations affiliated with the Jewish community had received special police surveillance; this morning, Guzman and Bordón were assigned to keep watch.

The building was the tallest on its block, a six-story structure with a black marble façade and bronze-framed double-glass doors. Above the entrance, the marble framed three vertical windows, and above these the four bronze letters were set into the stone: *AMIA*. Another six-story building occupied by textile importers stood to its left, and to its right, down to the corner with Viamonte, was a line of smaller shops and offices. The *Once* neighborhood, like Manhattan's Diamond District, was the traditional Jewish quarter of Buenos Aires. Though a growing number of Korean and Chinese families had arrived in recent years, taking over the fabric and textile stores, several synagogues, Jewish social clubs and theaters remained, and some prominent members of the religious community still lived in *Once*.

The AMIA building was full of activity on the morning of July 18. Security kept watch of the front doors, searching all bags or suspicious packages entering the building, and most of its four hundred and fifty employees were kept busy: workers at the Treasury on the second floor prepared documents for a meeting of the Board of Directors later that morning, while the rest of their department oversaw the cashier boxes, where debtors arrived to pay installments on their loans and insurance plans. Martin

AMIA before the attack

Cano, a waiter for the building, was also preparing for the board meeting, dragging his rolling table onto the basement elevator, laden with a heavy tank of fresh coffee. Mourners had lined up at the funeral department on the fourth floor, looking to provide their loved ones a traditional Jewish burial, while the unemployed gathered outside the employment offices. At that time, the Rec Center for the elderly and the Center of Jewish Documentation were perhaps the only places still empty. Otherwise, much of the building's administrative staff, with their offices on the upper floors closed for renovations, were stationed temporarily in the theater belowground.

The construction workers carted debris through the lobby to the entrance, where Guzman watched them emerge, ascend a makeshift wooden bridge, and empty their carts into the new dumpster on the curb. AMIA's Chief of Security, a former Israeli combatant, had ordered the dumpster moved a further two yards from the entrance, in the direction of Viamonte—an order which, though he could not have known it at the time, would prove fateful.

Just then a man knocked on Guzman's window and bent over to speak. He was a baker, delivering pastries to a shop across the street, and needed to double-park his van. From where he sat, Guzman could see the trays piled in the back of the van. The man's son was with him. Guzman waved, and just as father and son began their work, a silver car parked behind the van, appearing to suffer from mechanical issues. The driver stood at the opened hood, instructing one of his companions inside the car. Guzman knew the driver: he ran a print shop nearby. The car was filled with his materials. Guzman stepped out of the patrol car. He told the printer to hurry—two vehicles double-parked on such a busy street as Pasteur hindered the traffic considerably—and entered the Café Kaoba. The café was crowded, but he spotted an empty table at the far end of the room. "*Un cortado,*" he said to the girl behind the counter, and watched the street through the front window as he waited.

The baker and the printer were still parked outside; a janitor for the building facing AMIA looked on the scene as he washed down the sidewalk with a hose, and the municipal street sweeper passed by, pushing his trash barrow ahead of him, filling it with a mixture of garbage and mud from the sidewalk as he went. A mother walked quickly past, in the direction of Calle Tucuman, dragging her five-year-old son along by the arm. He trotted at her side, trying to keep up. She was glad they had caught the subway to the Pasteur station: they would be on time for the boy's kindergarten. She looked once more at her watch—9:53—and in the next instant felt an overpowering heat press upon her back.

Nobody really knows what happened next, but from various accounts we have gathered an idea of events.

Ana, a sociologist for AMIA, was on her way to the technical area on the second floor, to use one of the building's word processors, when the building began to shake uncontrollably. Pieces of masonry fell through the ceiling, a cacophony of shouts and shattering glass reverberated. Ana threw herself into a nearby emergency door, emerged onto the outdoor terrace, and climbed to an adjacent building, the sounds of terror pursuing her.

Hugo Fryszberg, in his office on the second floor of AMIA, would recall hearing not one, but two explosions, only a few seconds apart. At the first sound, Hugo's manager shouted, "Everybody under cover." Ducking beneath his desk, Hugo felt as though he were slipping into a deep abyss. After the second explosion had ended, he looked up and saw only darkness and smoke. An acrid smell filled the air; it was difficult to breath. Stumbling through the smoke, he met some colleagues, and joined them to rescue a woman whose desperate shouts arose from beneath the rubble. They carried her away, clambering up the debris to an adjacent balcony, and turned to survey the scene behind them. Hugo couldn't believe it: the AMIA building was gone; he could see the building to its rear through the space it left behind.

A video taken moments later shows people walking in shock

through a cloud of dust, vacant-eyed, their clothing shredded. Human remains litter the road; howls and cries mix with the calls of sirens, and the streets fill with a procession of ambulances and police cars. Glass had exploded from every window and door within a three-block radius. A lamp pole had been lifted from its place on Pasteur and stood imbedded in the cement at the corner of Viamonte, a hundred yards away. Rolls of fabric hung like tattered curtains from the broken windows of a warehouse on the corner.

The AMIA building itself had been reduced to rubble. Later, we would learn the reason for the sound of the second explosion, as Hugo heard it: the first had lifted the building into the air, which, falling back to  earth, produced a thunderous second roar. The sound of it was heard miles away; a mushroom cloud rose more than three hundred feet overhead.

Police and emergency services arrived several minutes after the explosion, and hundreds of civilians gathered on Pasteur. Gradually, the search for survivors began. Nobody was really in charge; a  confusion of emergency officials and volunteers searched for survivors amidst the rubble. Several orthodox Jews, dressed in their traditional attire, ascended the rubble. Policemen, firemen, and civilian volunteers made several chains of baskets: for cleaning debris, distributing water bottles, and later, sharing food. From time to time, people at the top of the pile shouted to the crowd below, demanding silence. They needed to hear whether somebody was calling to them from beneath the rubble.

One stretcher after another was pushed and dragged to the top of the pile.

Many people within the building—the laborers and the mourners, the unemployed and several of the AMIA staff—died instantly. Across the street, bits of debris had buffeted the baker  and the printer like bullets. Apart from the lucky ones, who found an immediate exit to an adjacent terrace or roof, the survivors of the AMIA staff were buried beneath the rubble and rescued several hours later—by which time many more died of the injuries sustained. News footage that evening showed emergency forces working to uncover a survivor, when a large piece of masonry hanging from the remaining foundations came loose and fell, crushing one fireman. The trapped man was rescued more than thirty hours later, but would die, too, in the ambulance.

Guzman and Bordón survived: the former was propelled through the rear wall of the Café Kaoba, into the men's restroom, while the patrol car's raised hood absorbed  much of the impact, miraculously protecting Bordón. The street sweeper fell into the empty dumpster and was found several hours later—in shock, but alive. In an apartment building on the other side of the block, a woman on the top floor returned home to find all of her furniture overturned; her small pet laying injured beneath her bed.

The injured were sent initially to nearby hospitals, and then redirected to more distant hospitals and other institutions as these overcrowded. No group oversaw this process. Nobody knew how many were injured. Logically, it must be presumed that when somebody was reported injured, he was within range of the explosion; but no testimonies were taken from these injured witnesses. Corpses and human remains were sent directly to the morgue, two blocks away, for identification. Many, however, were beyond recognition; even today, some remains rest unidentified.

The number of people killed in the explosion and its aftermath is estimated to be roughly eighty-six—however, because the terrorist who detonated the bomb is presumed among the dead, eighty-five is the more frequently cited number of victims. Still, no proper, systematic search for evidence was undertaken. The number of people injured was certainly more than four hundred, but even this figure cannot be seen as accurate.

After four days, authorities announced the arrival of a team of Israeli rescue forces and explosives experts to aid in the recovery and investigation. Twenty men arrived with two search dogs, but they had come too late to find any survivors in the rubble—whoever remained buried was surely dead by now. Yet the Israelis worked nonetheless, going over a separate section of the site, apart from the Argentine groups.

In the coming days, a group of journalists who visited the surrounding buildings, led by Jorge Lanata, collected several bags of debris and pieces of metal from the rooftops that investigators had yet to search.

One doorman called the police to inform them of human remains which, several days after the explosion, still littered his terrace. The resident of a building at the corner of Tucuman and Pasteur later described the remains that had affixed to the outside wall of his apartment, only to wash away, several weeks later, in the rain.

2
CORRUPTION

A national politician once referred to Argentina as a "mafia state"; Adolfo Perez Esquivel, winner of the Nobel Peace Prize, spoke of the society's predominant "moral illness". Neither is far from the truth. It is impossible to understand the AMIA bombing and the events to follow, without first understanding the corruption which has pervaded Argentine society—a political corruption which time and again we have forgiven, speaking the popular slogan: *They steal, but they do something.* In its current form, it is a cyclical corruption: a corrupt politician appoints a corrupt judge, who is in turn supported by corrupt members of the community. This corruption can likely be traced to the demagoguery of the first Perón administration, orchestrated effectively by Juan Peron and Evita. But there was a cultural tendency to corruption as well, visible amongst the lower and middle classes, which in most ways resulted from the simultaneous breakdown of the nation's economic and societal stability. Carlos Menem, who would be President in the 1990's, was later reported among the richest men in Argentina; if not for the collection of accountants and strawmen who (mostly) successfully veiled his true wealth, he might have been nominated to the

Forbes 500 list: an unexplained and extraneous Swiss bank account, discovered in his name, was found to contain US$ 700,000—pocket money, for him.

Juan Domingo Perón, "Isabelita" Martínez de Perón and José López Rega

Isabel Martínez, Juan Peron's third wife and Vice President during his third and final term, assumed the presidency in July 1974, following Juan Peron's death. Without real power and charisma, Isabel was largely controlled by Peron's former secondhand man and private secretary during the latter's exile in Madrid, Lopez Rega. Lopez Rega was known as *el Brujo*, the sorcerer, owing to his rumored interest in black magic—several rumors even identified himself and Perón as practitioners of occultism—as well as his great influence over the elderly Perón.

Isabelita as President after the death of Juan Perón, with López Rega

Once an obscure police sergeant, he had been inexplicably promoted to head of the Federal Police during Juan Perón's presidency, and, in the latter's final term, served as Minister for Social Welfare. In this time, he began secretly recruiting members of the security forces to root out guerilla members and sympathizers. During the interim presidency of Raúl Lastiri, he organized the AAA—the Argentine Anticommunist Alliance—a far-right paramilitary force which functioned effectively as a death squad, executing those suspected of collaboration with guerrilla forces and leftist groups. Their powers during Isabel's reign broadened, claiming several hundred lives in all. For many Peronists, it is still difficult to accept that such brutal repression was begun under Perón's own administration.

Nonetheless, it was only a foretaste of the ruthlessness to come: in 1976, Jorge Rafael Videla organized a *coup d'état*, overthrowing the Perón administration and establishing a dictatorship that would terrorize the country until 1983.

The Military Junta: Videla (center) Massera (far left) and Agosti (right)

Anyone who lived in Buenos Aires at that time will recall the green Ford Falcons used by the secret police, rifles and machine guns wagging through the open windows, passing freely through the city's traffic. Military forces were a common sight on the streets, arresting pedestrians

Green Falcons and "dirty war"

simply because they could not produce proper identification or explain their destinations. Videla organized the "Operational Groups," which—much like the AAA, and the Nazi *Einsatzgruppen* before them—targeted supposed enemies of the state: left-wing activists, trade unionists, artists, intellectuals, university students, and members of the Church. As happened in such Nazi operations as *Night and Fog*, dissenters vanished *en masse*, and their final whereabouts remain unknown to this day.

I worked then in a criminal tribunal in the San Isidro parish, twenty miles outside of downtown Buenos Aires. There were only three tribunals in San Isidro, each with two different clerks of the court, and each clerk directing a division of eight members, including one custodian, a policeman. Each division was assigned a mandatary shift every three months, for fifteen days. During each of these shifts, we received about five thousand cases—provincial tribunals in general, and San Isidro in particular, were overwhelmed with cases and detainees—and every time, without fail, several hundred of those were *habeas corpus* complaints concerning the *desaparecidos*: the "disappeared." Without computers, using only outdated mechanical typewriters suffering the interminable battery of the years, we notated testimonies, followed clues, typed and read, working at least twelve hours every day, seven days a week. Immediate notice was sent to the police and all security forces—the Army, the Navy and Air forces—but the response was always the same: *The requested person is not detained by our forces or being detained on any premises belonging to this Force.* Full stop, nothing more to say. There was little more evidence of these people's whereabouts, either because there were no witnesses, or whatever witnesses there had been were abducted, too, and so the appeal could not be ratified. The appeals ended where they had begun.

Eventually, we learned the extent of their torment: the *desaparecidos* were imprisoned in one of several detention centers, either in the provinces or within Buenos Aires itself, interrogated, and tortured in a variety of methods, including cigarette burns, starvation, electric shock

Repression against students

and sexual abuse. Many, with or without a final confession, were then tranquilized, loaded *en masse* onto a cargo plane, and dropped from above into the Río de la Plata. Bodies discovered on the shores of Argentina and Uruguay suggested what was happening, but it was not until the pilot of one of these flights confessed to a judge in Spain, several years later, that everything was finally bared to the public eye. In the meantime, it was no easy task to convince the Argentine people of the truth. Some simply could not accept it, stubbornly refusing even to consider that such horrors had occurred—were occurring still—within their own country; it would mean accepting their own complicity as well. Others, especially the right-wing groups, justified the so-called repression as a necessity of the "Dirty War," as they called it, pointing to the recent terrorist attacks against the security forces. It would take decades to shape public opinion, and even when disgust and a desire for justice became the common voice, the extremist rebuttals would continue to be heard.

Those many dark years left their mark on the country. During Isabel's presidency, we had the beginnings of Argentina's inflationary explosions that later would reach the top at the end of the first democratic presidency after the militaries; a "surviving-the-jungle" attitude became the norm: when inflation rates rise to over 600% each month, one becomes an expert in survival. People hurried to exchange their pesos for dollars, played loose with their credit, took out loans and became one link in a chain of unpaid debts—*la bicicleta*, as it is called in Argentina: I cannot pay you because my debtor cannot pay me because his debtor cannot pay him, and so on. A fluid, never-ending circle of debt. The public sphere is crowded with *ñoquis*: the name comes from a potato and semolina pasta meal, traditionally eaten on the 29th of every month to ensure good work and good fortune—the same day salaries are collected, and the only day the *ñoquis* show up for work.

Low salaries, too, led to corruption: a *Diego*—a ten-percent bribe—might convince city hall inspectors to look elsewhere; IRS employees might misplace a well-dotted dossier along one of their many corridors, and union organizers might choose to end their strike. There are retirees who have hardly worked a day, but receive a pension thanks to their friendship with a powerful politician. Cheating was the unspoken public policy: in school, on taxes, bills, and fines. Just look at the number of illegal electrical connections that exist in Buenos Aires; go to any downtown street, stand on any sidewalk, and you will see a cable strung from the electric meter to a kiosk, or to a neighboring workshop, or to a mobile food seller. A nearby doorman, having received his tip, will connect the building's electricity to the newspaper stand outside. Of course, let the shantytowns be; in those places, such duplicities are necessary to survive.

Only the loss of the Malvinas Islands to the UK in 1982 set Argentina back on its course to democracy. The loss reflected poorly on the military government, and widespread protest brought about its hasty collapse.

In 1983, following the first general elections in a decade, newly elected President Raúl Alfonsin commenced the historic Trial of the Juntas. A Commission of Notables selected more than seven hundred crimes out of the thousands perpetrated, tried the leading members of the dictatorship, and convicted nearly every one.

Alfonsin and returning to democracy – "Holy Week" military threat

After years of devastating totalitarian rule, not only within Argentina but throughout all of Latin America, this was a gigantic step forward. However, merely imprisoning a few of the chief military leaders was not sufficient justice. Hundreds of members of the military and security forces had also participated in the Operational Groups. Accordingly, proceed-

ings continued after the Trial of the Juntas, against all those who participated in that dark time of Argentine history.

In 1987, the economic situation began to worsen, and Alfonsin's popularity declined. At the same time, members of the military threatened with prosecution began a putsch during the Holy Week of that year. Alfonsin, a democratic but weak leader, succumbed to the military pressure and issued two laws to appease their leaders. The first was the "Final Stop Law," which fixed an expiration date on the prosecutions, up to which time—but at no time afterward—claims could be submitted. But Alfonsin and his staff had not anticipated the efforts of the several human rights attorneys, international organizations, and Argentine human rights groups, who together managed to produce a considerable number of claims before that date. These included more or less all the members of the military and the security forces suspected of perpetrating crimes during the dictatorship. Next was the "Due Obedience Law," under which it was presumed, unless proven otherwise, that all members of the security and military forces below the rank of Colonel had acted under the orders of their superiors, making their prosecution impossible. It was an outrage the Argentine public was not so willing to accept, especially after hearing the testimonies of the tortured victims. Alfonsin's lack of political vision was remarkable. Rather than replicate the resolution model employed by the King in Spain in 1981, when the right-wing militaries attempted their putsch in Madrid, Alfonsin that Holy Week preferred to consent to impunity.

As a result, these laws divided Argentina in two—a division which would not close for several years—between those who opposed immunity for such heinous crimes, and those who claimed it was time to close that sad chapter of our history, to allow our wounds to heal. The former group was labeled leftist, friends of the terrorists, and so on. The latter, consisting of many civilians who had contributed in some way to the dictatorship, by action or by inaction, consisted of so-called pacifists, who claimed to look to the future rather than the past. Of course, such things are never so black-and-white. It could be argued that Alfonsin had intended to avoid a civil war, to end public revolt against the military. But Argentina was eager for a return to democracy, and if the military did attempt a putsch they would not only suffer international isolation, but domestic repulsion as well. At such a moment, a real statesman would have understood, though the effort might cost some lives, that a true democracy needed to enforced.

These were difficult times. Democracy, put into doubt by the president's own actions, was not strong enough to quell the military threat. Alfonsin was pushed to forgive and forget; it was a bullied resolution. Certainly, those who do not learn their history are doomed to repeat it. Alfonsin lost a great deal of political support; worse, his economic measures were virulently protested, especially among the growing Peronist base, and his administration fell to one of the highest inflation rates in Argentine history. He did not even have sufficient time to conclude his mandate, and so passed the burden on to his successor.

Carlos Menem assumed office in 1989, and, though a Peronist, installed a pointedly right-wing liberal government. In one of his first major acts, he pardoned the junta leaders and participants who had already been sentenced. He pardoned the defendants, too, who were still awaiting trial—an astonishing decision, because under Argentine law a person cannot be pardoned until he or she has been convicted. This was but the first in a series of scandals and lingering questions that would shadow much of Menem's decade-long presidency.

Menem new President

In 1995, for instance, Economy Minister Domingo Cavallo

stated in an interview that "neither security nor justice" was to be found in Argentina. He went on to reveal that Secretary of State Carlos Corach, under instructions from President Menem, met regularly with some federal judges who were utterly obedient to the Executive Power. Once, when Cavallo and Corach were dining together, the Secretary of State wrote in a napkin a list of those "loyal" judges.

Menem with Cavallo and Corach

Napkin judges

Though the individuals' names were never published, the "napkin judges," as the press aptly titled them, sullied the reputation of the government.

However, among the greatest crises suffered during Menem's rule were doubtlessly the terror attacks: the first, in 1992, against the Israeli Embassy—the first known attack of its sort in all of Argentina's history—and the second, two years later, against AMIA. Of course, the country was hardly prepared for such an attack in 1992: there was little surveillance at the borders, and security protocols were ill-defined at best; the ease of illegal entry had already made Argentina a popular destination for fleeing Nazi war criminals. The attack claimed the lives of nine Israeli diplomats, as well as the elderly residents of a building facing the Embassy, passers-by, workers, and several children from a nearby kindergarten. After the requisite clean-up of the attack site and initial inquiries,

Menem assigned Federal Police to observe Jewish institutions in the city on a rotating shift schedule, and assigned a political ally to command Frontier Control—a partisan decision that was his habit, and did little to effect meaningful change. Beyond these points, his actions were minimal. Security at the borders hardly improved. Investigations into the attack itself were near nonexistent: alternate theories held that the bomb had either exploded within the building, perhaps smuggled in with the crew working on renovations, or—and this was the explanation provided in the government's official report—had exploded on the street, from within a vehicle. Yet no surviving security footage could identify the vehicle used, nor narrow to any degree the methods of the attack. Until today several questions remain open concerning whether it was a terrorist attack or an implosion of explosives stocked at their own Embassy, as concluded in the report produced in the fall of 1996 by the Argentine National Academy of Engineers at the request of the Supreme Court. Nevertheless, rumors reproduced by some newspapers explained the bombings as a punishment directed to Menem for not fulfilling promises to the Syrian president Hafez El Assad in exchange for the Syrian economic support of Menem's presidential campaign. Others believed the bomb a reprisal for Argentina's participation in the Desert Storm Operation. To explain the Israeli government's apparent lack of concern over the attack, word spread that the Mossad had already identified the perpetrators and, secretly, eliminated them. Regardless, inquiries ceased, the case stagnated and wound up buried in a stray drawer of the Supreme Court. To this day, no answers have been provided.

By 1994, few effective measures had been taken to prevent a second attack.

3
NAZIS IN ARGENTINA

Argentina, like the United States, grew up and developed through an intertwined net of immigrants, whose descendants constituted the vast majority of the current population. These two nations, together with Brazil and Canada were among the few options for most European immigrants at the end of the nineteenth and beginning of the twentieth centuries. Each covered a vast territory, with manifold opportunities for skilled laborers. It was unsurprising that, amid poverty, drought, insufficient resources, sparse crops and political persecution in their home countries, the New World shone as a hopeful alternative. The impact of immigration was enormous: Argentina rose from a population of 50,000 in 1816, to 8 million less than a century later.

The Argentine Constitution explicitly affirms a duty to foster European immigrants, and a great number of Italian and Spanish immigrants came to form the country's population. In Europe, marriage between Italians and Spaniards was uncommon, separated as the two peoples are by France and two distinct mountain chains. In Argentina, however, such marriages became rather commonplace; the common Latin and Mediterranean heritage of those people were an attractive factor.

Containing such a variety of nationalities and races, all imaginable weather conditions, and a good net of railways and routes, adaptation was easy for a foreigner in Argentina. A number of Armenian, Syrian, and Lebanese immigrants settled in the north of Argentina, where the mountains and deserts surrounding the cities maintained some resemblance to the homes they had left behind—though the climate was, in fact, milder. An important group of Jewish immigrants went to the east of Argentina, especially to the Entre Ríos province, where they established various colonies. But a consistent group remained and was integrated into Buenos Aires, where they developed a powerful and wealthy community—at one time the second largest outside of Israel, after the United States. Although certain immigrants brought with them an anti-Semitism typical of Europe, the new country and customs obliged them to leave behind most such attitudes of discrimination. Tradition and religion were not an issue in the young Argentina. Of course, there were exceptions on both sides. A Jewish family would have some hesitations should a relative choose to marry a non-Jewish person, and the same could be said of the opposite case, should a member of the Catholic majority marry a Jew. Nonetheless, such marriages happened frequently, and caused no great fuss.

And yet, despite this image of an integrated society, the poisonous seed of anti-Semitism, favored by the surge of right-wing movements, had been always present. Anti-Semitic slogans and propaganda, isolated attacks against Jewish citizens, and defilements of Jewish cemeteries occasionally made the news. Things were clearly different during the time of the dictatorship, when, as happens in every right-wing government, anti-Semitism was evident. Survivors of the torture chambers at the ESMA and other concentration camps witnessed the particular discrimination, insult and abuse of the Jewish prisoners. Even in a democracy, those who have chosen a military career know well enough, though the military denies any form of discrimination, that there has never been a general of Jewish descent in all the history of the nation—and likely will not be for some time to come.

In 1987, Attorney General D'Alessio appointed me, as an expert in German and international law, to the extradition case of Josef Schwammberger, a former SS commander. Schwammberger was by then an apparently harmless, frail old man, but his actions during World War II had been horrific. From 1942 to 1944, he commanded three different concentration camps in Poland: Przemysl, Rozwadow, and Mielec. When the British arrested him, they discovered among his possessions several bags of cash and valuables, stolen from the prisoners he had personally helped to execute. After three years of confinement in various Allied military prisons, Schwammberger escaped, and, along with such prominent Nazi officials as Mengele and Eichmann, arrived in Argentina, with thanks to the ODESSA network —the Organization of Former SS Members (*Organization Der Ehemaligen SS-Angehörigen*)—and the lenient immigration policies of President Juan Perón. In the 1960's he received Argentine citizenship under a false name, settled in the suburbs of Buenos Aires, and found work at a petrochemical plant. After some time, he left Buenos Aires, whereupon his track was lost.

Josef Schwammberger

The Simon Wiesenthal Center, an international Jewish human rights organization with headquarters in Los Angeles, alerted the prosecutor in Stuttgart of Schwammberger's whereabouts in Argentina, who then offered a reward for further information. Sometime later, an anonymous caller revealed that

Schwammberger was in Córdoba, seven hundred miles from Buenos Aires, where he was soon arrested. The German government requested his extradition in 1976, but proceedings were slow in those days; Argentina had extradited only one Nazi up to then. Schwammberger's official crime was "homicide," and in Argentina homicide, like any other criminal offense, is subject to the statute of limitations: legal action must be taken within a defined period of time from the date of the crime—in this case, thirty years. After such a time, the right to prosecution expires; which in this circumstance, placing Schwammberger's crimes in 1944, had been the case. It is fair to say that international public law has evolved considerably since Schwammberger's case; today, such crimes against humanity are not confined by any statute of limitation. Yet in 1987 these ideas were still a part of the legal avant-garde in Argentina. Convincing the rather conservative judges—several of whom were appointed under the dictatorship — was not going to be easy.

The Federal Republic of Germany had extended the statute of limitations on crimes against humanity in order to extend the expiration of proceedings against Nazi war criminals, and later, declared those crimes not subject to any statute of limitations. But Schwammberger's case presented another legal difficulty, the dread of any international jurist: his private counselor contended that the Federal Republic of Germany had no rights to require his extradition because his client had been serving the German Empire—the Third Reich—which, at the time of the request, had ceased to exist. Germany had since divided into two different States, the Federal Republic of Germany and the German Democratic Republic, and according to the counselor, neither state could rightly be considered the successor of the former German Empire. This issue had been a central concern of the Federal Republic of Germany since the end of the war; its conclusion would have consequences relevant to the payment of indemnities to war victims—the Jewish people in particular. But, I had an ace up my sleeve for this argument: when I was working on my PhD in Germany, my thesis advisor was Professor Georg Ress, author of the most important book on the subject in all of Germany.

In order to resolve these contentions, I required a good number of documents and articles not available in Buenos Aires, when the Internet was nonexistent and fax machines were not yet commonplace. My request for assistance in retrieving these documents from the German government was seen by some, including such interested Jewish and human rights organizations as B'nai Brith, as an obstruction tactic. Representatives of these groups visited me—among them Emilio Mignone, a courageous human rights fighter—in order to see that my request was not merely an excuse to delay the process. They were wrong in their presumptions; the documents were necessary to answer my affidavit. I was able to obtain most of them from friends and contacts in Germany, and the German Embassy provided the rest. When I received all of the required materials, my affidavit was ready within two months.

My work proved that the Federal Republic of Germany could be seen as the political reorganization of the Third Reich, and that Schwammberger's crimes were not subject to the statute of limitations. With these arguments, the case was resolved within the trial court and the Court of Appeals. Attorney General D'Alessio fully accepted my position—though he suggested a couple of pages of my report, wherein I suggested that such crimes against humanity as those perpetrated by Schwammberger are under no statute of limitations, should be deleted. Clearly, being D'Alessio as General Attorney, the legal representative of the government and being a member of the same political party of Alfonsin, such suggestion conspired against both controversial laws of Final Stop and Due Obeyance. I published those pages separately in a juridical magazine, which would be quoted a decade later in the prosecutions of members of the Argentine military. Finally, after more than four years, Schwammberger was extradited.

Schwammberger remained in prison for fourteen years; until, on December 4, 2004, at the age of ninety-two, he passed away. Justice, perhaps, was late, but justice had arrived nonetheless. This was to become a leading case, igniting a revolution in criminal justice in Argentina and finally restricting impunity for grave crimes—such as those suffered during Argentina's own dictatorship. Because of my work in that case, years later the Italian Government would appoint me as it representative for the extradition of another Nazi: Erich Priebke.

In early May 1994, ABC News correspondent Sam Donaldson, following a prior investigation of the Simon Wiesenthal Center, located Erich Priebke in the city of Bariloche, more than a thousand miles south of Buenos Aires. Bariloche is a wonderful

Erich Priebke

place, surrounded by high mountains and beautiful lakes, a kind of Austrian or Bavarian landscape, but wilder and vaster. Donaldson was looking for Nazis in the south of Argentina, and approached a German resident named Juan Maler on the street. Maler's real name was Reinhard Kops, a former member of the SS intelligence service working in Rome during the German occupation. When Donaldson produced a photo of Kops in SS uniform, the latter said he was not important, that many people helped the Nazis there. The questions went on, and Kops began to look very worried. Then he brought Donaldson apart far from the camera, though the microphone was still on. He whispered that the real "big fish" was another German living there, and he mentioned the man's name in a very low voice. "Who," asked

Donaldson. Kops, hiding his face from the camera, murmured, "Priebke. Erich Priebke."

In 1944, Priebke was a young Captain of the SS serving in Rome. Rome was then an "open city," having abandoned all defensive preparations with the expectation that enemy forces would desist their attacks, in the interest of preserving the city's historic landmarks. Thus, a section of the SS Regiment Bozen was taken rather by surprise when a group of Italian partisans planted a bomb in a trash container in the center of the city, near Via Veneto. The bomb exploded as the regiment passed through a nearby alley, killing thirty-three of their members. Hitler himself, when informed of the attack, ordered that the whole neighborhood be razed to the ground. However, the German highest authority in Italy, General Kesselring, later changed the order: ten Italian civilians were to be killed for each of the thirty-three German soldiers, totally three-hundred and thirty victims. After all, Italy and the Third Reich were still allies. Yet Priebke, with the help of Pietro Caruso, Rome's Chief of Police at the time, collected three-hundred and thirty-five individuals. They were passersby, prisoners from all-Roman prisons, as well as Jews from the Roman Ghetto, near the *Circo Marcello*. Five additional hostages were taken simply because they were there. The hostages were taken to the nearby Ardeatine caves. Five at a time, they were bound, escorted into the caves, and shot in the back of the head. Witnesses later confirmed that Priebke himself had executed at least two of the hostages.

Donaldson finally located Priebke as the latter approached his car: "Mr. Priebke. Sam Donaldson of American Television." Priebke didn't appear surprised, and responded in English: "Yes, yes... What's for?" Donaldson asked if he had been in the Gestapo in Rome in 1944. Priebke vacillated and answered, "Yes," though he had never in fact been a member of the Gestapo.

After some questioning, Priebke explained the massacre: "You know, the Communists blew up a group of our German soldiers. For every German soldier, ten Italians had to die."

Donaldson asked, "Civilians?"

"Well, civilians ... there have been ... mostly terrorists." He denied having executed children, and went on: "That was our order. You know? The war. Those kinds of things happened, you know?" He insisted that he had been following orders, and affirmed that he didn't shoot anybody. After another moment, Priebke realized he had put himself in an uncomfortable situation. Stepping into his car, he told Donaldson, "You are not a gentleman," and shut the door.

Sam Donaldson with Erich Priebke

In 1978, I lived for a couple of weeks in Rome, in a small hotel at Via Rasella, just a few yards from the place where the bomb against the Bozen regiment had exploded—though, of course, I did not know it at that time. A remarkable coincidence, Rome being such a large city, that I was lodged in that very same alley, only two short blocks long. A hundred times I walked that alley. Only when I returned to the place in 1994 did I see the evidence of that blast, the still-present scars on the walls surrounding the upper windows. It surprised me that I had not seen them before. The sunlight tanning the red ochre roofs that October afternoon struck those irregular holes made fifty years earlier, when the surviving soldiers fired their

Via Rasella

guns overhead in confusion, presuming the attack to have come from above.

The discovery of a perpetrator of the Ardeatine massacre shook the Italian government. What was worse, Priebke was not hidden; he was not even using a different name, and was found rather easily by a curious journalist. He had transformed himself into a kind of philanthropist in Bariloche; he had founded and directed the German school there; he was a respected member of the community. Even the Italian honorary consul in Bariloche was is friend and partner. Human rights organizations and Jewish groups in Italy, along with those elsewhere, increased political pressure, demanding that Priebke be brought to trial. Italy requested his extradition from Argentina, and Priebke was immediately arrested.

However, nothing was simple in his case. Priebke selected as his legal counselor Pedro Bianchi, a well-known right-wing criminal lawyer. In the Trial of the Juntas, Bianchi had defended former Admiral Emilio Eduardo Massera, a leading participant in the dictatorship and purported mastermind of the "disappearances."

Bianchi loved interviews, and immediately informed the press that the case has expired under the statute of limitations and that he would require a huge amount of evidence should the extradition request proceed to trial. These documents and cases, he stated, would need to be certified authentic by the corresponding authorities and duly translated into Spanish. It was clear that his request was only meant to slow the proceedings, to make Priebke's extradition impossible, or, considering his advanced age, futile.

In accordance with Argentine law, the local National Prosecutor officially represents any foreign government in an extradition case; but, as I did not want to give Priebke's attorney the time to appeal my appointment, I was acting in this case as the Italian government's legal advisor, directing the prosecutor on his next actions.

The first obstacle was the statute of limitations in Argentine law. Fifty years had elapsed since Priebke's participation in the massacre; if he was charged with murder, the thirty-year statute of limitations would apply, and extradition under Argentine law would be impossible. My initial instinct was to repeat the arguments of the Schwammberger case: crimes against humanity are beyond any statute of limitation. But the Argentine Criminal Code had not yet institutionalized such crimes. Even the Italian authorities had characterized Priebke's crimes in their request as "war crimes", which, like "crimes against humanity," were not included in the Argentine Criminal Code. According to the legal principle of specificity, an act must fit into the precise description of a crime in order to be charged as such. I had the burden of arguing the validity of my own legal theory: certain crimes are so malignant they attack not only the state where the crime is perpetrated, but the whole of mankind, and are not resolved simply by the passing of time. I had to convince not only the prosecutor of this, but, more importantly, the judge himself.

I met the prosecutor in Bariloche, a young fellow, one of several fresh attorneys leading the force of federal justice in their city. He was decent enough to inform me that he would follow my instructions as a representative of the Italian government, though he personally disagreed with my position: after fifty years, he believed, the statute of limitations had set in; the right to legal action had expired. The prosecutor and I tried, alongside our Italian colleagues, to devise a common strategy.

In addition to our concerns over Bianchi's efforts at obstruction and the potential expiration of the statute of limitations, we were concerned that Priebke would argue the defense oft-heard in such cases: that he was only following the orders of his superior. This argument would have an additional weight with regard to war-time reprisals, in which case a Captain of the SS would not have the definitive word. Herbert Kappler, head of the SS in Rome and commanding officer of Priebke, had been prosecuted and imprisoned in Italy many years before, though he escaped in 1977 and died the following year.

Indeed, the order had in fact come from above: ten civilians were to be executed for each of the thirty-three German soldiers killed. But three hundred and thirty-five victims were killed in the Ardeatine massacre, five more than the number required by Kesselring. As I considered the matter further, the significance of this discrepancy struck me: Priebke could not claim those five additional executions were a part of Kesselring's orders; for these, he had no excuse. This presented the opportunity to argue that Priebke had murdered of his own volition, if only these five, not merely to appease his superiors. Then, as I read through the list of the executed I learned that many of them, seventy-five exactly, were Jewish.

Herber Kappler

Looking into the archives, I saw that Priebke and Police Chief Caruso, without instruction or explanation, had retrieved certain of these victims from the Jewish quarter—"il ghetto," as the Romans called the old houses near *Circo Marcello*, in the neighborhood of the Campo dei Fiori. The former issue was possibly only the result of a miscalculation; or else one of the German soldiers, nervous to ensure that the correct number was gathered, had mistakenly gathered five too many. Regardless, this did not

The execution of Pietro Caruso after the war

explain the selection of Jewish victims; it was clear these had been selected merely for being Jews.

The court denied Bianchi's request for evidence, and the Federal judge conceded the extradition; Bianchi immediately appealed the decision. Now the case was not to be decided in Bariloche, but elsewhere, where the Federal Chamber of Appeals has its seat. The whole story would repeat there, and it seemed Bianchi would appeal and re-appeal any measure in order to obtain the delay he wanted. In the appeal instance, the new prosecutor was a great ally, arguing that crimes against humanity in fact deserved punishment beyond the statute of limitations of the Criminal Code.

I returned to Buenos Aires with some expectations. In spite of which, my worst fear was suddenly realized, when, some days later, the Chamber of Appeals reversed the decision of the judge of Bariloche and denied Priebke's extradition to Italy. The statute of limitations, they said, had expired. The press announced that Bianchi had organized a banquet in Bariloche when Priebke was freed.

I perfectly recall that day. When I heard the news on the radio, it was like receiving a heavy blow to the chest. I left my apartment and began to roam. I needed to think. I found myself in Recoleta Cemetery, among the graves of Argentina's most famous citizens, small ornate edifices like those in New Orleans and Paris.

I phoned the Italian Ambassador and urged him to arrange for me an immediate appointment with the Argentine Minister of Justice, who, that same evening, was by chance flying to Rome. The Minister's office was not far from the cemetery, and by the time the appointment was arranged I was already waiting on the sidewalk in front of the building. The Minister, Rodolfo Barra, was at that time a very powerful man. Sometime later, a journal would publish photos of him as a fourteen-year-old member of the student branch of Tacuara, a pro-Nazi group active in the

1960's, and his reputation would duly suffer. At the time of our meeting, however, his reaction to my problem was very positive. I informed him of the manner in which the Chamber of Appeals had freed Priebke, and formally requested he bring the case to the Supreme Court. He was a clever man, and he realized immediately the significance of this case for Argentine-Italian relations. He instructed the General Attorney to appeal to the highest tribunal.

After the meeting, I ran to the Italian Embassy. On the second floor, everybody was upset. The television had shown Priebke with Bianchi, both of them smiling. Bianchi said the Italian Prime Minister was "inept", and the next day this quotation appeared on the front page of all the major journals in Italy. But, again, I had a hidden card up my sleeve. I phoned the German consul from the office of the Italian Ambassador. I had represented Germany in several other extradition cases, and I knew the Germans would be interested in extraditing Priebke. They only needed to request extradition by a so-called "verbal note", sent to the Argentine Foreign Office as soon as possible. This would allow the Argentine government to arrest Priebke immediately, to show some good will toward Italy. Germany would have thirty days to present the formal extradition request, though I hoped to reverse the Chamber of Appeals' decision first.

It worked. Bianchi's smile would last just one hour. The German government promptly requested Priebke's extradition, and he was arrested once again. This time he would not be released: the Supreme Court reversed the decision of the Chamber of Appeals. Priebke was extradited to Italy, where, after a difficult trial, he was sentenced to life in prison.

Because of my success in this case, I would later aid the prosecution in another major investigation in Argentine history: the AMIA bombing.

4

MEMORIA ACTIVA

In October 1995, owing to my past success in the Schwammberger and Priebke cases, the Argentine representative of the Simon Wiesenthal Center introduced me to a group of those affected by the AMIA bombing: forty people, many Jewish families, most of them parents, spouses, or siblings of the deceased. As such, they could together assume a role in the criminal proceeding similar to that of the prosecutor. They could consent to, discuss, or appeal any one of the judge's decisions, even when the prosecutor has already consented. And, too, public opinion is typically in the victim's favor—an advantage which, in the AMIA case, would be of paramount importance.

Two Argentine-Jewish institutions officially represented the group: AMIA, of course; and DAIA, the Delegation of Argentine Israeli Associations. Perhaps the most important Jewish institution in Argentina, DAIA had its offices on the fifth floor of the destroyed AMIA building. Its president, Ruben Beraja, would take an active role in the AMIA case, expressly supporting the official version of the investigation. Beraja was also the president of Banco Mayo, in whose headquarters he maintained his private offices, and vice president of the World Jewish Council, which earned him considerable renown throughout the Jewish community.

Yet the group was dismayed with the impassivity of the lead investigators, and their representatives, they said, were too acquiescent. "They just repeat what Galeano says," a tiny woman told me. "They are totally uncritical."

She referred to Juan José Galeano, a court clerk who, owing less to merit than to an acquaintance with the State Secretary, Carlos Corach, had recently been promoted to federal judge. He was an *arriviste*, a social climber, a "napkin judge," and had first become renowned, in May 1994, for his prosecution of a detainee on the charge of theft, after the man ate the lunch of one of Galeano's employees. Known as the "sandwichide," the case demanded a lengthy written proceeding, dictating the accounts of several eyewitnesses. On July 18 Galeano was on duty, and so, in the aftermath of the AMIA bombing, was assigned to lead the investigation.

Judge Galeano

President Menem, in order to minimize whatever blame might be directed at his administration, worked to affect the appearance of efficiency: he announced that updates on the investigation would be made public daily, and provided Galeano a model tribunal, with a team of expert investigators and security forces, and the most advanced technology at their disposal. Among the tribunal's most envied pieces of technology was the Excalibur, a brand-new and highly expensive software allowing intertwined conversations between different cell-phone callers.

The tribunal was not to investigate anything but the bombing—Galeano's would be the only federal tribunal focused on a single case. His entire team, all the employees and policemen under his command, would be exclusively devoted to this. Additional personnel were added to the court after the first year, reaching numbers unprecedented in most tribunals.

Despite these provisions, the lack of progress in the AMIA case was not surprising, if one recalled the ineptitude and corruption of investigators following the Embassy bombing. From whatever evidence had been collected, they could say only that a white Renault Trafic van, probably driving along Pasteur, had rocketed into the entrance of the AMIA building, detonating more than a thousand pounds of explosives. Yet none of the several witnesses to survive the explosion had seen any such vehicle approach the AMIA building. On July 25, seven days after the bombing, it was announced that the engine of the van had been found among the rubble of the AMIA building. According to the written acts of the judicial proceedings, which constituted public documents under Argentine law, a policeman spotted the engine among the rubble gathered with a hydraulic excavator; the machine operator was immediately ordered to stop, just before he emptied his load into a container of debris.

The Renault Trafic model used for the attack

Yet the clean-up of the site, the group explained, was simply irresponsible. All the rubble and debris, collected in trucks, had been deposited on an open, hundred-acre tract of land alongside the Río de la Plata, between the Jorge Newbery Airfield and several departments of the University of Buenos Aires. At first, the trucks deposited their contents in piles numbered according to the order of their arrival. Then someone forgot to take note of the successive arrivals, and the trucks continued pouring their contents without organization or concern. When the Jewish community later organized a more detailed search of the dump site, identity documents and pieces of cloth, books from the AMIA library, even human remains were found. The wire fence surrounding the perimeter was loose in several places, and over time surveillance of the area waned; police custody was waived, and collectors began taking from the piles of rubble; pieces of the AMIA building appeared on the streets of Buenos Aires, sold as souvenirs. In 1996, the piles would be gathered again, in a clean-up of the land. Following a judicial decree, all the rubble was finally pushed into the river, in a horrific display of stupidity, inhumanity and indifference.

An aerial view of the land tract where the debris of AMIA were poured, and later removed into the river. The Ciudad Universitaria is seen at the end (Photo Argentine Federal Police)

I hesitated to take their case. My knowledge of the bombing and its investigation was only gleaned from the press reports—which, unsurprisingly, were not very revealing. What I knew was that the bombing was a racist crime, and I was not a member of the victimized group; I was and still am a Catholic. I explained that if they were to hire me as their legal advisor, it might be perceived as an insult to the Jewish community and the institutions representing them. I learned later that my hesitations were not one-sided: the majority of the group, too, had been reluctant to meet with me.

A few days later, I received a phone call from a member of the group, informing me they had chosen Elias Neuman, a respected Jewish criminal attorney, as their representative. I expressed my satisfaction at their selection; I assured them they would be in good hands.

. . .

And so they were—until, two years later, I received a second phone call: their attorneys had resigned.

Early in May 1997, I met with three representatives of the group: Diana Malamud, Laura Ginsberg, and Norma Lew, each of whom had lost a loved one in the bombing, and now each voiced their defense of the victims' families.

Diana Malamud

Norma Lew

Diana's husband was the architect of the AMIA building's renovations, while Laura's husband had been one of the top employees in AMIA's Funeral Direction on the fourth floor; each was a mother of two, and each left now to raise their children alone. Norma I remembered from the meeting two years earlier: she had lost her son, and was now the president of Memoria Activa, an organization founded within a few days of the bombing. Translated literally as "active memory," in truth of meaning the title more closely suggests a "persistent memory," an unceasing search for justice and a refusal to forget—a purpose, an intent in their remembrance.

Memoria Activa was composed of survivors, along with friends and relatives, with the aim of preserving these events within the popular, public consciousness. Every Monday, Memoria Activa and its supporters gathering in Plaza Lavalle, facing the main doors of the Palace of Justice, seat of the Supreme Court. Located in the *Tribunales* neighborhood—

Meetings in Plaza Lavalle

so called for the many national courts located there—Plaza Lavalle was more typically known for the few dozen booksellers who set their booths in the square.

At exactly 9:53 AM, two members would blow the *shofar*, a trumpet made of a ram's horn which, in traditional Jewish ceremonies, signals combat. This improvised pulpit earned them national attention; at least one news channel was present at every gathering.

Shofar in Memoria Activa meeting

Yet they were losing faith. DAIA and AMIA were proceeding as private prosecutors, and every time the women proposed a new investigative strategy, they were impeded by Ruben Beraja and his attorney, who discouraged criticism. "They told me I was a traitor *hija de puta*," Diana said. "Can you believe it? My husband died there! They are using us for their own political benefit."

They could see little difference between what these organizations claimed and the "official version" offered by Galeano and the government: the AMIA bombing was a terrorist attack, and they spared no means in their search for those responsible.

Yet, Diana said, the investigators offered few developments since the attack. Galeano's work was suspect: he had flown to Venezuela, they said, with the stated purpose of meeting an Iranian repentant with information on the bombing, then returned to Argentina and announced to the press: "You are going

AMIA victims monument in Plaza Lavalle

to be taken aback when you learn the truth." After visiting Menem at his residence in Olivos, however, Galeano never spoke another word on the matter. Surprisingly, nobody protested this open liaison between Galeano and Menem, a clear violation of the necessary independence that should prevail within the judiciary branch. Then, on the issue of four Iranian diplomats who were rumored to have been involved in the bombing, he neither took action nor made comment. Every time they visited Galeano, he was kind, offering them coffee and cookies. But he did nothing for the case, which Laura proclaimed "a cover-up by Menem and [Vice President] Duhalde."

They pointed to Wilson dos Santos, the Brazilian citizen who, early in July of 1994, tried to warn of an imminent terrorist attack against an Israeli organization in Argentina, first at the Israeli Consulate in Milan, and then at the Argentine Consulate. The story he told seemed more fitting to a Robert Ludlum thriller: a conspiracy centering on Iranian terrorists and weapons dealers, as well as an Iranian prostitute with whom dos Santos had been traveling throughout Europe. Yet, despite the outlandishness of the story, dos Santos was correct about one fact in particular: the objective was a Jewish or Israeli organization in Buenos Aires. After the explosion, the police in Buenos Aires even received an international telephone call from dos Santos: "I told you that this was going to happen," he said. Notwithstanding the reality or unreality of dos Santos' story, it should at the least have been reported, but the Argentine Consulate simply rejected the information without consideration, and only after the bomb the matter was informed.

Wilson dos Santos (right)

"Why was Dos Santos dismissed without taking any

measures?" asked Norma. "Something definitely wrong is happening with the investigation."

Despite the little demonstrable progress on the case, whenever the anniversary of the bombing approached, a grandiloquent announcement would be made—Beraja would say he approved of Galeano's investigation, he approved of the prosecution's work so far. He said the truth was well-hidden, but the greatest efforts were being made to uncover it; he claimed the Secretary of Intelligence and his team worked side-by-side with Galeano. He said we had to believe in the real efforts of these people, working day and night, with only AMIA in mind. We should trust Galeano; he and his skilled associates were gathering thousands upon thousands of documents. We only had to be patient.

Hearing their complaints, whatever hesitation I had felt was gone. I was prepared to take the case, despite the contrary advice of my friends and colleagues. But I could not be hasty.

"Why did your attorney resign?" I asked. They looked at each other. Elias Neuman was a brilliant criminal law professor. I had read his books on criminal sociology as a law student at the University of Buenos Aires, and again when I began teaching criminal law. "Neuman does not want to carry our case anymore," was all Norma would say. I ended our meeting, promising I would consider their case after first speaking with Neuman.

When I called him, Neuman would only affirm that he was determined to resign. He was fed up with the judge, he said; fed up with his fellow attorneys, with the Jewish community in general and with his clients in particular—absolutely fed up with the case. "It's over," he said. I tried my best to convince him to remain, at least until I could take over for him. He wished me luck— "All possible luck"—but he was done.

Later that week, I met with Laura, Diana, and Norma again. I accepted their case. At the time, I was comfortable enough to dismiss compensation. They would pay a monthly fee to cover my expenses, collected from Memoria Activa's funds, but I represented the three women personally as a separate party.

On July 18, 1997, Laura was to speak at a gathering on Pasteur to commemorate the third anniversary of the bombing. In one of my first actions as their representative, I received her speech to proofread. It was strong, but they feared potential consequences. In one part of the speech, Laura made reference to Menem and Duhalde; but she did not accuse them directly, despite her certainty of their complicity. I encouraged Laura to say what she pleased. I suggested she use Emile Zola's famous declaration from the Dreyfuss case—*J'accusse*—and I assured her I would handle whatever consequences arose.

Laura Ginsberg

The anniversary was as cold and grey a morning as three years before. An impressive crowd gathered along Pasteur, where a small platform and several microphones were set up, with a tent overhead to protect from the rain. Carlos Corach was present—he, too, was Jewish—as well as Jorge Rodriquez, the Chief of the Cabinet. The crowd held up photos of the victims, and long black banners hung from sidewalk to sidewalk over the street, with the legend in white script: *Today we all are Memoria Activa*.

Laura ascended the platform, began to speak, and paused, looking out beyond the cameras at the multitudes before her. Then, she began in earnest:

I close my eyes and imagine it is July 18, 1994, seven in the morning. We wake as we do every Monday to begin the week. Parents share breakfast with their children, and all say, "I love you," before going out. But many of us did not, because we could not have imagined it was going to be the last time.

I close my eyes and imagine it is that 18th of July at ten in the morning. Monica and Felix go to work; Romina, to the university; Jorge brings coffee to a client, and Sebastian, only five years old, continues walking with his mother along Pasteur Street. None of them will reach their destination.

I open my eyes and the image of that horror invades me: smoke, firefighters, police, people pushing, people crying, people screaming, people praying, people unable to do anything, not cry nor scream nor even curse. Seven minutes before ten, the AMIA building has been blown away.

The speech continues with this rhythm, like waves hitting the pier, bringing the audience to the idyllic dream of what should have been—*I close my eyes to the beloved world*—and crashing them into the truth of reality: *When I open my eyes, I see the devastation.*

She continued in this way, closing her eyes, recalling the victims' final moments:

But when I open them, I find myself three years later, listening to the declarations of the Minister of the Interior, Carlos Corach, boasting of having apportioned economic resources for the reconstruction of the AMIA building and having subsidized the families of the victims, as if this should have something to do with resolving the attack.

Corach, behind her, was pale. The other officials looked as though caught out of place. Laura continued, speaking more quickly and with a heightened passion.

I close my eyes and imagine it is four in the afternoon, that 18th of July. The kids return from school, take a snack, turn on the television and the broadcast is normal, without rubble or death. But when I open them, I find myself three years later, when nothing has been done about President Menem's famous, supposed Iranian contact, nothing has been done about the four Iranian diplomats who could never be interrogated, and the Minister of Exterior Relations has done nothing, absolutely nothing, about the previous announcement of the Brazilian

Wilson Dos Santos, who anticipated the attack before the Argentine Consul in Milan at the beginning of July 1994.

Then she rose to a climax, whereupon she pronounced the following sentences, striking the country like an electric shock:

All crimes and attacks committed and yet to come have a common denominator: I accuse the government of Menem and Duhalde of consenting to impunity, of consenting to the indifference of those who know and keep quiet, of consenting to insecurity, to unskillfulness and to ineptitude. I accuse the government of Menem and Duhalde of covering up the local connection, which helped to kill our loved ones.

The crowd was enraptured; her declarations had awakened them. They roared in applause. They shouted, calling Corach, Martinez, and all the members of the government "murderers". Rubén Beraja followed as speaker, but the public rebuked him, jeering at every word he spoke. He and the other directors of AMIA and DAIA would later visit the Casa Rosada, the President's official residence, to apologize for Laura's words.

That was the only gathering I attended in remembrance of the bombing, though they have recurred every July 18 until the present day. I recall afterward I began to walk to my office, three miles from Pasteur. I was distracted and anxious, thinking of the great battle to come. Memoria Activa was just a small group, no more than three dozen altogether, confronting the powerful machinery of the government and the larger Jewish community. I could not help but recall my conversation with Neuman; I had had the feeling, after hanging up the phone, that he had wanted to tell me something, to warn me of something, but finally could not.

5

THE TAPE

I was introduced to Galeano the same day I submitted my request to be the new private prosecutor for the three women of Memoria Activa. Laura and Diana had warned me I would not get anything from the judge; he was a hypocrite, and they were fed up with his unfulfilled promises. Despite their protests, despite everything I had learned from the newspapers—the *sandwichcide*, the "napkin judges"—I saw it as my professional duty to give Galeano the opportunity to prove his integrity. And, too, I worried Galeano might reject my application to represent Memoria Activa; if tempted to eliminate opposition, he might claim AMIA and DAIA sufficiently represented the Jewish community and the victims, and that no further parties were necessary. There was no sense in fighting him from the start.

Galeano was in his mid-thirties, five foot eight, thin, with a gray flannel suit, manicured hands pinned at the wrist with cufflinks, wearing a ten-day beard and a balding head of hair.

Somebody told me we had attended the same college, a Roman Catholic institution called Colegio de La Salle where I spent twelve years, and we spoke casually of the school, about the teachers we had shared. I carefully avoided problematic questions. I offered my full collaboration, showing that I held no prejudices against him. I told Galeano I was reading the AMIA case from the beginning, and would be very thankful if he could provide photocopies of the remaining volumes.

I knew there were, at the time, as many as two hundred and seventy volumes directly related the case, but Galeano then informed me of nearly three hundred more focusing on parallel investigations, such as one devoted to the case's connections with arm dealers. At that time, I didn't think much of these "parallel investigations," but they would be a strong problem in the future.

We talked for thirty minutes, without speaking of anything in particular. After all, I was the victims' representative, and it was widely known that my clients were very dissatisfied after three years of empty investigation. It was clear, despite whatever camaraderie we derived from our schooldays, that Galeano was facing the representative of his worst critics. The tension was palpable. But after the country-wide shock of Laura's speech, and the crowd's open hostility to Beraja, any attempt to challenge Memoria Activa needed to be carefully considered if he did not want to risk another scandal.

In Argentina, at that time, the judge was the king of the courtroom; he decides what is admissible and inadmissible. However, these decisions cannot be arbitrary or whimsical, and cannot affect the rights of the defense. The judge, according to penal proceedings, makes the final decision as to whether the accused should be prosecuted, and when. This system is different from the United States', wherein the judge is totally impartial and must be convinced. In Argentina, the judge may have his own ideas, and the parties might be surprised with a development only conceived within the judge's mind. In this way, the judge drives the proceedings, and the prosecutor and the defense work as his auxiliaries.

It was clear from the beginning that Galeano preferred the practices of Argentina's intelligence services, SIDE—the *Secretaría de Inteligencia de Estado*—and would not care much for the transparency of the legal proceeding. He decided early on to work with a near intervention of the Secretary of Intelligence and to form attached annexes to the main written proceeding, with the supposed objective of investigating those clues that did not deserve to be considered in the principal. However, as well as protecting his investigation from an inquisitive prosecutor, these secret annexes gave him total freedom to determine the content, extent, and significance of those texts. This freedom was reflected in Galeano's actions through the proceedings: not only did he decide not to investigate certain facts and events, but he modified the proceeding and made decisions that would most benefit his own supposed needs. For instance, he resolved the parties' requests through a declaration of the phrase *téngase presente*, or *be it known*. Not a refusal to allow the party to appeal, neither was it approval of the party's proposal, leaving the final decision of when and how the requested measure would be accomplished - if that was ever going to happen - to Galeano himself. Whenever a request fell outside of Galeano's plans, or threatened to clarify the murky road he was paving, *téngase presente* could stall the entire investigation.

In 1996, with the second anniversary of the AMIA attack approaching, the investigation was still not advancing as fast as the public demanded.

The discovery of the Trafic van's engine had been a decisive moment. The registration numbers engraved in the engine's motor block, when traced, led investigators to the official owner of the vehicle: Messin SA, a merchandising

Renault Trafic van

firm dealing in cloths and fabrics. It seems Messin used the vehicle, a white Renault Trafic van with rear doors, carrying two identification plates numbered 1.498.506, to deliver to its clients. In March 1994, for unknown reasons, the van caught fire in the closed lot where it was parked, destroying its cargo, money, and documents before the firemen could arrive to extinguish it.

Yet it was not until the discovery of the last known van's possessor, Carlos Telleldin, that events began to take shape. Telleldin himself was a known crook, with a history of theft, smuggling, and other such crimes - nothing significant, but he had earned jail-time nonetheless. He was identified as the last holder of the van on July 28, days after the engine was discovered on Pasteur. Though it was doubtful that Telleldin or his wife Ana Boragni had participated in the bombing, it seemed he knew perfectly well who had been the last possessor of the van.

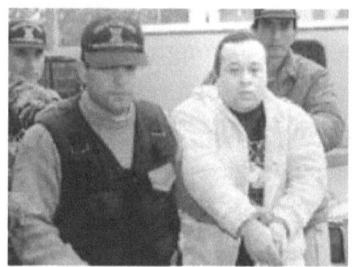

Carlos Telleldin

A certain Perez, who was present at the time, agree that when news of the explosion aired on television, Telleldin turned deathly pale and began to curse. He left his home and went into hiding. Accounts of the following days differ, but one thing is certain: a couple of

Telleldin and his wife Ana Boragni

days later, he arrived in Posadas, south of Iguazú Falls, near the Triple Frontier at the junction of Argentina, Brazil, and Paraguay. From Posadas, he phoned his home in Olivos, where SIDE was already waiting. Fortunate for Telleldin, a couple of policemen answered; they were in business with Telleldin and his wife, though they claimed to be working undercover. They convinced Telleldin to turn himself in to the police at the Aeroparque Jorge Newbery, the domestic airport within the Buenos Aires city limits.

He arrived on July 27, on a flight from Posadas, the capital of a Northeastern province near the Brazilian border, and was immediately placed into custody. He was brought to the Federal Police Department, in the center of Buenos Aires. Among his possessions at the time of arrest was an electronic agenda. It would never be seen again. At the same time, a search party was dispatched to his home in Olivos, where his personal computer, as well as multiple agendas, a telephone book, photo albums, and PC diskettes were seized. This was, at least, what the search report stated, though the diskettes and photo albums had also disappeared. The computer's hard drive was never introduced into the proceedings. A couple of years later, these materials were returned to Telleldin without any further investigation.

Later still, the more than sixty tapes containing conversations between Telleldin and intelligence agents, recorded prior to Telleldin's surrender, disappeared inexplicably, both from the Central Police Station, and from the Secretary of Intelligence, elsewhere in Buenos Aires, where they were supposedly being investigated. The official explanation was that they were reused, and Telleldin's conversations were taped over. It was said to be a coincidence that both institutions did so simultaneously.

As it turned out, Telleldin in fact ran a whole organization specializing in "car duplication." The son of a well-known torturer during the times of the military dictatorship in Córdoba, five hundred miles from Buenos Aires, he had always walked along the dark side of the road; many details of his life were indeed sordid. He once owned a night club, as well as several brothels in different apartments in Buenos Aires, where even his own wife, the mother of his children, worked as a prostitute. He tried to breed pigs, to manage a video club, to rent an island in the Buenos Aires waterfront, to sell boats and motorbikes, but nothing worked. He was the sort who needed always to be engaged in some dubious activity, but inevitably grew bored—or else found the profits insufficient—and finally moved on to something else. He had several run-ins with the police for selling stolen cars and goods, but after bribing the officers he earned their forgetfulness each time. This borderline existence won him some powerful friends and allies, who would be helpful to him later on.

At the time of the AMIA bombing he was established in Olivos, a pleasant residential quarter in the province of Buenos Aires, close to the Presidential Residence. He managed a car wash, doubling as a duplication site, and he concentrated on selling his duplicates, particularly Renault Trafic vans. The Trafic van was a short, utilitarian vehicle, very suitable for transporting cargo, and more manageable than a full-sized truck on the many congested streets of Buenos Aires. With time, Telleldin had prepared a good team of forgers and mechanics; his business was booming. The Buenos Aires police, infamous for their corruption, posed him no problem he couldn't resolve with a bribe.

The duplication worked as follows: when a vehicle was burnt in an accidental fire, the owner would call the insurance company. If the inspection of the sinister fell within some insurance inspectors, who worked in league with some dubious car dealers, would arrive and confirm the damages but for an amount far below the insured price of the vehicle. Of course, the owner would be disappointed; his premium would not be enough to cover the price of a replacement vehicle. Then, the inspector would play his joker: if the owner sold the remains of the vehicle to a certain car dealer that he knows called Monjo, who specialized in such damages, Monjo would pay the rest of the money. Then, with both the insurance premium and the difference paid by Monjo, the owner could afford a brand-new vehicle. Now everybody would be happy: the insurance company, which paid a reduced premium on a fully insured vehicle; the owner of the vehicle, who received the promised amount; and the insurance inspector, who received payment from Monjo. Monjo would then offer the burned vehicle to Telleldin, or else to another suspicious car dealer. It was a carcass with an engine, but it came with clean papers. Theoretically, according to Monjo, they would repair the vehicle and sell it refurbished. Telleldin, however, had other plans more convenient to him than an expensive repair: he would steal a model similar to the one he'd bought from Monjo, install the engine from the purchased vehicle into the stolen one, forge the chassis registration numbers, and bring the duplicated vehicle to the open market. Telleldin would publish an ad in the classified section of a newspaper known for advertising second-hand cars, and, if anybody was interested, a meeting would be arranged. If the chassis of the original vehicle was not totally destroyed in the fire, he may even request a new set of registration papers to sell the engine of the stolen vehicle with the chassis of the original. These alterations were so finely done that any duplicated vehicle could pass the official exam with the Car's Registration Office, allowing the purchaser to obtain whatever documents were lost in the fire.

He bought the remains of the Trafic van in Monjo's parking lot, and brought it to his workshop on July 4, 1994, along with several other vehicles. He immediately contacted his friends, Fernandez, Jaimes, and Cotoras, and gave them the details on the van. Fernandez was to steal a similar model, while Telleldin's wife Ana would transport the van's engine to the duplication site. With Cotoras's help, Telleldin would then insert the engine into the body of the stolen vehicle—engines are numbered in the block, and so are very difficult, even impossible, to copy. Jaimes would erase and re-engrave the number on the chassis of the vehicle—his skill at this had earned him the nickname of "surgeon"—and, with the papers for Messin's van, they would have assembled a brand-new Trafic van for the price of the remains. The main reason for Jaimes' accuracy according to the acts, was the laser pencil he used, the same used by Renault in the vehicle's original manufacture. The result was so perfect, Telleldin then brought the van to the official Cars Verification System of the National Registry of Vehicles, where, after the Registry verified the vehicle, he was issued new documentation for the car. The engine of the stolen car was used for spare parts, and the numbered block, was destroyed in a scrap yard. One week later, on the 9th and 10th of July 1994, the van was listed in the classified section of *Clarin*, a popular newspaper.

Under interrogation, Telleldin's tactic was to couch his fabrications in smaller bits of truth. He gave correct addresses, but not the most recent ones; he pointed out accomplices, but mixed up their names. In describing how the van was built, he truthfully explained how he had received the engine, but he lied about how he had obtained the chassis—taking the story from another case, in which he had intervened a few days earlier. The investigators followed his clues, and they arrived at very confusing conclusions: Telleldin was right about the chassis, but it seemed this chassis didn't have a side door, as the one used in the AMIA bombing did. On the other hand, the accomplices who worked on the chassis agreed with Telleldin on some details, but differed over others. The result was a mess of information, which the investigators did little to sort out.

Before Galeano, Telleldin gave several accounts of the final sale of this van. In his first declaration, he claimed the purchaser was a Colombian named Ramón Martínez, who paid US $10,000 in cash. He even produced a bill of sale, wherein the sale of the van was registered, although the buyer declared a non-existent address, and the listed ID number 47,372,118 did not match the numbers used for foreigners at that time in Argentina. He mentioned that he even tried to visit Martinez after the sale and invoked the name of one accomplice. Telleldin altered his own ID, too: in place of the double-l in his last name, he had inserted a double-c. He had used this trick to hide his whereabouts before. In the bill of sale, then, Telleldin appeared as "Teccedin." He even told investigators that, as he was absentminded, he had forgotten to give Martínez the so-called "green card" necessary to operate a vehicle in Buenos Aires, and that when he went to the address Martínez had given him, nobody there had ever heard of such a name—though Martínez is as common a name as there is in Argentina, much like Smith or Miller in the United States.

Then, the man was Chinese.

Then, one week later, Telleldin changed his account entirely. He claimed that on July 15, he had a meeting with an attorney provided by the police. The attorney informed Telleldin that the police were looking for him; they knew he was involved in car theft, and they were asking for US $90,000 in order to continue his work. But that story, too, was dismissed. In October, Telleldin decided to take up a hunger strike over his living conditions. Soon after, he was relocated to another prison. Telleldin's last declaration contained pieces of the truth. He had in fact been arrested earlier in 1994, while having an affair with a young girl named Sandra. The two lovers were interrogated; Sandra, in tears, claimed she knew nothing of Telleldin's activities, and Telleldin finally consented to pay US $90,000, as well as give up a motorbike and boat.

In July 1996, after two years in jail, the story was revisited. Galeano summoned Telleldin to his offices, and the latter, with Galeano's support, accused that same group of police officers from the Province of Buenos Aires. According to this newer testimony, several officers of the South Brigade, under the command of Juan José Ribelli, a Buenos Aires sheriff also known as *el Zorro*, had arrested Telleldin several months prior to the AMIA bombing. They demanded he pay US $90,000, he said, under threat of imprisonment for his illegal activities. Of course, he accepted. It was pocket money: he could make that much selling cars in just two weekends. Yet only a part was paid in cash. The remainder was paid with different properties, including a motorbike, a worthless piece of land, an island on the mouth of the Río de la Plata, and a car: according to this version, the Trafic van. Shortly after his declaration, Ribelli and the rest of the policemen involved were set up and arrested by their own superiors.

In Argentina, the summer holiday is a serious matter, especially for the country's judicial workers: during the whole month of January, the tribunals close their doors. The inhabitants of Buenos Aires travel to the ocean, to the long yellow beaches in the province, 250 miles from the city, or, if they are wealthier, to the chic Mediterranean-style resort city of Punta del Este, crossing the wide Río de la Plata into Uruguay. The press, eager to entertain its beach readers, is attentive to every minor incident this season.

In the summer of 1997, newspapers and tabloids were delighted with the romance between attorney Mariano Cuneo and a young woman named Samantha Farjat. They first met through a police case that combined all the elements of a front-page story: famous athletes, sex, drugs, betrayal, and corruption. The case included soccer star Diego Maradona, then recovering from a well-publicized drug addiction, along with his manager at the time, Guillermo Coppola, a famous face in the Argentine media, and another member of the 1978 world championship team. Its lead actresses were three promiscuous girls, Samantha the most notorious among them.

After the police arrested Natalia's boyfriend under suspicion of drug dealing, acting judge Hernán Bernasconi, greedy for fame —which he would later attain when he was impeached and incarcerated for his illegal proceedings in this case—together with several corrupt officers of the Narcotic Division of the Federal Police, trapped the three girls. According to Samantha's testimony, the officers then threatened to prosecute the girls for drug-dealing, unless they "helped the investigation"—specifically, demanding that they plant drugs in the homes of Coppola and soccer star Tarantini during the orgies they hosted.

Coppola's attorney, the handsome, blue-eyed Mariano Cuneo, eventually convinced Samantha to change her testimony and admit the truth. Cuneo also sought fame and public recognition, and this was the perfect scandal for a lazy summer. The sexual parties had included two of the most prominent members of Bernasconi's police squad, Diamante and Gerace, and everything was presented in a sensationalized television program, which included a hair-pulling fight between Natalia and Samantha. The story shocked the hypocritical and prudish Argentine society. A new slang word emerged in Argentina: *"samanthización,"* or, to becloud the path, to muddy the fields, to confuse or obscure; to tell a lie so colossal as to finally distort the truth.

Cover weekly magazing with Samantha Farjat and Ribelli's Counsellor, Mariano Cúneo Libarona

Samantha's change in testimony and the scandal that followed acquitted Coppola and Samantha's former boyfriend of the accusations. A few weeks later, Cuneo abandoned his pregnant wife for the summer, travelling to Brazil with Samantha. Now he was "the attorney of the stars," and the scandal brought him, as anticipated, to the front page.

Samantha Farjat and Natalia Denegri

In the middle of his affair with Samantha, on March 10, 1997, Mariano Cuneo was called to take the defense of Juan José Ribelli. This was the kind of case Cuneo wanted. His fame and success at the time was already earning him comparisons with Robert Shapiro and Johnny Cochran.

Juan José Ribelli

Shortly after taking the case, Cuneo delivered to his client a package he had supposedly received by mail. Ribelli then requested an interview with Judge Galeano, and brought with him the contents of the package: a gift-wrapped videotape. Ribelli, who had already watched the video, said it was a "present" the judge should watch alone.

The tape contained footage from the cameras Galeano had ordered set up within the court, with the help of SIDE. The footage showed Galeano meeting with Telleldin, offering him US $400,000 for information.

It was a scandal beyond proportions.

The tape proved several things: first, it proved Galeano had bribed the prime suspect of the gravest terrorist attack in the history of Argentina. Secondly, Galeano had recorded the accused without informing him or the parties involved. Finally, Galeano kept the tape in his office safe, which meant somebody close to him—either an employee of the tribunal or a member of the secret services—had stolen the tape and passed it on to Cuneo, or more probably, directly to Ribelli.

It was clear Ribelli was threatening to make the tape public if Galeano proceeded with the case against him and his men. Galeano called the Prosecutors Muellen and Barbaccia, and informed them of the taping; they too had participated in the recording, had even filmed their own interrogations in the prosecutor's offices, and they, too, appeared in the footage.

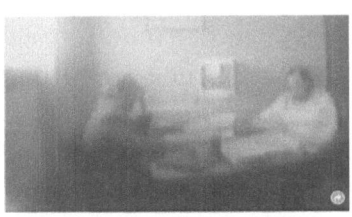

Video of the judge Galeano handling with Telleldin

Everybody was surprised. The tribunal was being blackmailed; it would be difficult to avoid publicity. Galeano and his associates decided upon the only possible exit: they made the issue public, and another federal judge was appointed to investigate the extortion. The new judge, Oyarbide, was also a "napkin judge," and the following year would himself be the subject of a videotape scandal, when footage of his homosexual encounter in a brothel was released, and the edited footage shown on television. He filed charges against Ribelli and ordered Cuneo's telephone lines be tapped. Cuneo, however, had already given copies of the video to the press. They accepted them with some reluctance: AMIA was a major case, and the consequences of making this public were unpredictable. The attorney Pablo Jacoby, who would serve later as my co-counselor to Memoria Activa, then represented a well-known journalist, Jorge Lanata, who had received a copy of the video and decided to air it during his program. Pablo remembered those days very well, running back and forth with copies of the tape, evading seizure by the Argentine police and intelligence services. Finally, his client aired the video. This was to be the first of numerous unprecedented scandals relating to the AMIA case.

In the meantime, Galeano contacted Ruben Beraja and AMIA's attorney, Luis Dobniewsky. They had already seen the tape in question. They were informed of some facts Galeano didn't reveal to the legal counselors of the defendants, and later would not reveal to Memoria Activa. Galeano also contacted the Embassy of Israel and the Congressional Investigative Commission in charge of the AMIA bombing.

Oyarbide ordered the arrest of Cuneo and his partners under charge of aggravated extortion. Cuneo spent two weeks in jail. After his release, he resigned from Ribelli's case.

Several years later, Melchor Cruchaga, a member of the Investigative Commission, admitted they were wrong at the time, but explained that everybody had been determined to defend Galeano and the AMIA investigation at all costs. Thus Galeano escaped from his crime, and was stronger for it. He came to believe he was invincible, and he would soon make efforts to prove it.

6

READING

In 1997, legal proceedings in the Argentine federal courts were divided in two main parts: the first was written, with the investigating judge acting—theoretically—as a neutral arbiter, collecting evidence that should have been useful to either party. The parties could only suggest measures for obtaining evidence, documents, or testimonies, but the final decision remained in the hands of the judge, who was free to refuse their proposals without further explanation. He "owned" the proceeding, and exercised full control over the direction of the investigation. If the judge was fair, the case would proceed smoothly; it was unlikely an appropriate request would be refused. On the other hand, when a judge held preformed opinions or submitted to the influence of parties internal or external to the case, the situation could become complicated.

Accordingly, after investigation, the judge might conclude that all evidence related to the case had been collected. When this occurred, he might decide to end the proceedings, either prosecuting or else closing the case without indictment. There was another alternative that would later be crucial to the AMIA case: the judge might declare that a suspect was not worth further investigation. In such a case, the judge issued a statement of "lack of merits"—*falta de mérito*— which placed that person in a limbo, a gray zone, whereupon the parties were impeded from further action. Theoretically, the goal of such a situation was to pause the investigation until a further conclusion could be made, either discontinuing the case or affecting the charge for an indictment. Yet the amount of time allowed for this decision depended exclusively upon the judge. This could be especially problematic if, for whatever reason, the judge did not want to continue the investigation, yet also wanted to avoid the protest of the opposing parties. Placing the pertinent person under *falta de mérito* would in fact protect this person from subpoena. The manner in which this declaration factored into the AMIA case caused us considerable issue. For example, Ana, Telleldin's wife, was named, before my arrival to the case, a person with "lack of merit," which meant —although Telleldin's confessed that his wife had transported the engine, and although this confession had been used to prosecute Telleldin himself—I was unable to interrogate her, neither as suspect nor witness, in all my time with the AMIA case.

When I was appointed as private prosecutor to Memoria Activa, the investigation carried out so far by Galeano numbered about two hundred seventy volumes— equivalent to fifty-four thousand pages. However, only Galeano  knew the real number of volumes. The lack of control was certainly suspicious. Galeano had gone far beyond the limits of the law. The thought of seizing the investigation from the control of the parties involved was unheard-of in the Argentine Code of Criminal Procedures, and in a normal case such an action would have resulted in the nullification of the entire proceeding. But in the AMIA case, of course, everything seemed to favor the investigative preferences of Judge Galeano. He had also implemented a witness protection program, a procedural institution then unknown in Argentina, which should have opened new lines of investigation. Although in theory these witnesses should have provided the court with vital information, nothing of the sort happened; on the contrary, Galeano seemed to use the program to hide witnesses from the parties.

In order to fully understand the development of the case up to my appointment, then, I had to read—just for a start—those fifty-four thousand pages, to which Galeano was theoretically adding new pages every day. I soon realized at least two incomplete proceedings needed to be added, too, each containing more than one hundred volumes. It was an extraordinary amount of reading, and the task seemed to me impossible in the time given. I also had to obtain photocopies of the coming volumes. When I assumed my position, the previous attorney for Memoria Activa had nearly forty of these volumes on his person. I organized a schedule to obtain particular photocopies every day, in order to follow along with the documents the tribunal was handling. This would prove to be extremely difficult in the succeeding months.

Yet I had an advantage in my task: the San Isidro tribunal where I worked in the 1970's produced more than three hundred and sixty verdicts each month, a hundred and eighty from either division or Secretaries. This was in addition to the daily investigations, the verbal accounts of witnesses and suspects, the administrative work, the visits to jails around the province, and so on. I would design for the less important cases—such as when the perpetrator had confessed his crime and requested only some leniency—a one-page, two-sided verdict complying with all formal requirements of the Code of Criminal Procedure. But it had to be typed on one of the battered Olivetti typewriters, with multiple copies. That way at least six verdicts would be produced every day of the month, along with the testimonies, the convictions or releases, the answer to the pleadings of the prosecution and the defense, the attention to evidence, the collection of documents, information, forms, or whatever else might be required for the case, as well as the tribunal's administrative paperwork.

I worked every day from 7a.m. to 7p.m., or 8p.m., or 9—but as a young law student I felt I was contributing to some greater justice. I discovered horrible things: individuals imprisoned several years for unproven crimes—or, worse, accusations of which they were clearly innocent. But I hadn't created this system of justice; I hadn't appointed the incompetent judges to their seats. I was merely working within the system, and I was committed to doing my best in order to restore justice to any case in my hands. I worked eight years in San Isidro, and in such circumstances, as one might imagine, I learned to read faster, to distinguish between the important and the unimportant clauses, to unearth among all that information the concrete facts and essential evidence. These skills would be considerable assets to my reading of the AMIA case.

Whenever an attorney wished to see the written acts of the case, this would take place at the *mesa de entradas*, a front desk at an open window, where the attorney can read the case under an employee's supervision. AMIA and DAIA may check the case comfortably inside the tribunal for this purpose. In the years to come, I would read the documents standing at this very front desk. It was a tradition I humbly accepted, and kept to through all my years on the case.

I set out to read at least ten volumes of the photocopies provided each day, something like two thousand pages legal-size. Now that I recall my first efforts, I realize it was my commitment to read the whole proceeding and take notes, make an index, and double-check testimonies that made the difference. A normal reader would simply refuse to read such a mountain of legal lingo and would try to concentrate, if possible, on the major declarations, witnesses, and so on—which alone would have taken a considerable amount of time. I read everything, from telegrams to communications, to the tribunal and police notes.

I began from the first page, a transcription of information received from the Federal Police Department, describing an explosion of extraordinary power in Barrio Once. The document was a mess. From the site of the explosion, the investigation moved to concentrate instead on two German tourists who "looked suspicious." This search, however, proved a waste of time. Immediately afterward, investigators with the National Police suspected some Arabic-speaking people in a building near AMIA; then, a taxi driver who dropped a couple off at AMIA to take pictures, and so on. Nothing in these lines of investigation suggested any clear, logical direction. It might have made more sense to check the immigration authorities' lists for recent arrivals from the Middle East, but nobody cared to do so. At the least, they ought to have conducted a more thorough search of the rubble at the bomb site, for further evidence of the exploded van, or whatever else might have survived.

The subsequent pages were documents from the City Morgue, concerning the arrival of ambulances carrying human remains: ten, twenty, forty or more bodies. Hospitals received the injured survivors: ten, one hundred, two hundred, three hundred individuals. An initial list of the recognized victims was produced only several days after the blast. Then the documents spoke of the turmoil and confusion in the aftermath of the explosion, the victims, relatives searching for their loved ones, the efforts of the Federal Police to contain the growing number of volunteers helping in the search for survivors. Everything was there, despite the misspellings, the outdated typewriters, the insensible forms. The AMIA investigation followed no logical direction.

Yet I read relentlessly, feverishly, at every opportunity, wherever I could. I read quickly, oblivious to the rest of the world. I read at home, in my office, throughout the lunch and dinner hours. I began carrying a couple of volumes every time I went out to eat, and an unfinished volume rested near my bed when I slept. The completed volumes began to pile up in my living room, near the telephone, on the shelves of my bookcase. I exhausted my yellow markers every three days. I had to develop a system of symbols to keep track of my discoveries, or else I marked the page, folding it as I did in the courts, folding it diagonally once and again, leaving the corner sticking out.

After the first days of constant reading, I realized an index would be necessary to collect my notes and comments on the finished pages—as well as, more important still, to collect the evidence that Galeano and his team had not yet gathered. Memoria Activa provided me two typists to copy the pertinent parts of the texts I had already marked, an accurate system for crosschecking information and verifying the different witness accounts. Thus, my office was transformed into a collection of typists on several different computers, each preparing indexes to one volume at a time, all of which would be finally compiled in a cumulative index. The system proved effective. For example, I would on occasion discover that evidence relating to a particular witness was lacking. I would mark the page with yellow marker, highlighting the witness' name or the title of the document, and the typists would add a symbol at the beginning of the index, allowing them to gather all similar marks later on, when preparing the first request for further evidence. In this way, we were also able to crosscheck names and locations and other miscellaneous facts, and to verify that a request made in the

Judge Juan José Galeano

early volumes had been carried out—or had not—in the later ones.

I soon realized the most elementary evidence was lacking. Much of it was there, waiting to be collected, yet after three years had not been produced. In 1997, Galeano was focused entirely on the AMIA case, even SIDE and the Federal Police were working under his directives. Yet the investigation had stalled. The prosecutors representing AMIA and DAIA should have been interested in shining a light on the case, and indicting anybody complicit in the attack. Yet they contributed willfully to Galeano's "official version" of the case. This could be seen from the very beginning, when their representatives encouraged the future founders of Memoria Activa to allow some flexibility of the rules, in order to separate the important developments from the other aimless paths, ideas, investigations, and clues arising with the passage of time. Their reasoning did little to justify a blatant violation of due process, but it was decided before my appointment; before I could pass any judgments, I first needed to learn all I could about the case.

There were several mysteries. On page 114 in the first volume of the judicial acts, for instance, the Director of Investigations requested Galeano's authorization to tap several dozen phone lines, for which he provided only the telephone numbers. Surprisingly, though the document lacked a date and signature, it was placed among the acts dated from the 20th to 21st of July 1994. But what made this document unique—such that 114 became a somewhat mythic number during the proceedings—was the fact that among the listed phone numbers were Telleldin's, his brother's, and his mother's. The engine linking Telleldin to the AMIA case would not be discovered until several days later, on July 25. Something was wrong here. Over the years, a number of investigations would be undertaken concerning page 114, but none could discover the truth. The most widely accepted explanation was a leak by SIDE. The page was photocopied and given to one of the private prosecutors, without correcting its mistakes. Nobody had properly controlled the written proceeding, and page 114 showed its potential meaning later on, when it was already too late to correct the page number or to make the page simply disappear.

It was clear Galeano and the government did not intend to perform a true investigation. They were simply collecting data, with neither sense nor intention. For instance: a man in Ushuaia, at the southernmost point of Argentina, more than four thousand miles from Buenos Aires, stated to the police that he had been involved in the AMIA bombing. After his declaration, a medical exam confirmed the man was mentally unstable and suffered from paranoia. What did Galeano do with that? Easy: he sent five investigative groups to the south to gather one thousand pages of written text and photos of the madman, to record lengthy interviews with local witnesses relating to his story, to draw up diagrams of the place the man lived, checking and re-checking everything the witnesses had said, and after expending several thousand dollars in lodging, fuel, and tickets, they concluded again that the individual in question was mentally unstable and suffered from paranoia. I was convinced I was either facing a case of blatant incompetence, or else it was a cover-up beyond all possible imagination.

Again and again, these escapades from the main proceeding interrupted our research, wasted our time and used up our daily thousand-page quote of photocopies from the tribunal. One day, we received a volume of photocopies of dollar bills, and that was repeated with the next two volumes. Just bills that had been seized by Monjo, the car dealer. Later we learned that among those photocopies, an act has been introduced declaring the lack of merits of one implicated. But even that act didn't appear in our copies. It was clear, wasting time was an objective; the evidence pointing to this began to pile up.

Among the most important pieces of evidence lacking in the

AMIA case was the bodywork of the vehicle used for detonating the bomb. We know today that the engine first belonged to a firm named "Messin"; next was sold to Monjo, and then to Telleldin. But we don't know until today to whom belonged the chassis of the van built by Telleldin.

Pieces of the van were dispersed across the site of the explosion; an effort at retrieval was made, yet a photo shows the scraps that were left behind, forever reminding the viewer of the incompetence and ineptitude exhibited by the investigators. The bodywork was lost forever. The destiny of the remainder of Messin's van is equally unknown. The only piece ever recovered was the engine. But what remained of the vehicle's bodywork was enough to prove they corresponded to a different model. Accordingly, it seemed Telleldin or somebody related to him had installed the engine of the original burnt car from Messin into another body. The Messin's van, for example, had only back doors, while the model discovered after the bombing had an additional lateral door. Telleldin gave several contradictory accounts of the bodywork used to install the engine. None of them corresponded with the scraps recovered from the AMIA building.

Prosecutors Muellen and Barbaccia

When one compares the few recovered scraps of the van with the recovery of TWA Flight 800, exploded eight miles from Rhode Island in July of 1996, the results are devastating: Argentine authorities recovered less than 10% of the body of the Renault Trafic van, and not one piece of it helped them to identify the original

These were the only parts of the Trafic found at the AMIA place

owner, while American efforts resulted in the recovery of 85% of the destroyed aircraft.

There was the issue, too, of the sacks of dirt presumed to have been in the van, piled up around the bomb, serving as a sort of cannon barrel to project the explosion in a particular direction—much like in the barrel of a cannon. Samples were found at the site of the explosion, but after three years no analysis of that soil had yet been performed.

Another failing of the investigation was the lack of research done into the possible owner of the body of the van. Nobody had checked the garages located near Telleldin's home, or checked for other stolen vans in the city or the province. Flipping through Telleldin's agendas, I discovered that several names and numbers in his address book had been cut out with scissors, clearly after they had been seized. One of the agendas, however, contained the number of somebody identified as *tapicero*: upholsterer. If the van had once been burned, presumably the seats had been reupholstered. I assumed in that case Telleldin had reused the body of the van, and installed the engine of the stolen one. That circumstance deserved, at the least, some investigation. Accordingly, I added all these points to the list of my requests.

Another mystery persists concerning Santa Rita, the demolition company which owned a container at the blast site, and Santa Rita's owner, Nassif Haddad. Haddad also possessed a quarry where TNT had been used. After a Santa Rita truck driver left the empty container at AMIA, just minutes before the explosion, he continued to another address in Buenos Aires, and left another container on an empty plot of land belonging to J. Kanoore Edul, a Syrian with connections to both President Menem and the gun dealer Mozer Al Kazar. Searching Kanoore's cell phone history, investigators pinpointed a call dated earlier in July, just a week prior to the explosion, to Carlos Telleldin. Kanoore Edul was, or so it seemed to be related to the van. All of this seemed, at the least, a surprising coincidence. Kanoore was now a suspect. He was, however, related to President Menem's brother, and when Memoria Activa asked to subpoena him for interrogation, Galeano simply refused their request with a *téngase presente*.

It was unclear how many cars were parked on the same block as the AMIA building. The number would have helped to determine how the Renault Trafic van had managed to climb the pavement in front of the building and detonate its bomb. The AMIA building's security guards, established in all prominent Jewish buildings after the 1992 attack on the Israeli Embassy, could not explain how the cars were parked along the sidewalk or say with any certainty that there was enough space to pass through. Around this time, the journalist Jorge Lanata, published a book asserting that the bomb was placed in the Santa Rita waste container, and that the van never existed. On the other hand, Nassif Haddad, the owner of Santa Rita, also owned a mine, and for the purpose of this latter venture had purchased large quantities of explosives. Haddad insisted he never once brought explosives to his firm, where the waste container was picked up; yet a report of the Explosive Brigade of the Federal Police found traces of explosive material in the firm's main building in Buenos Aires. Nobody cared. I also discovered, double-checking the witness accounts, another car had been parked that morning near the AMIA building, and yet the tribunal had performed no further investigation to identify the vehicle or its driver, who had departed shortly before the explosion.

Investigators did discover that a white Renault Trafic van had been parked on July 15, three days before the explosion, in a parking lot a few blocks from the AMIA building. The lot attendants remembered the van for several reasons: first, its motor had stalled while entering the lot. The driver tried several times to restart the engine, without success. He exited the vehicle and glanced at the car behind him, as though asking for help. Then the occupant of that car exited his vehicle, approached the driver's seat of the van, and immediately the engine worked again. This second person parked the vehicle in a far corner, against the wall. The attendants recalled this incident because it all appeared so well-coordinated, they thought they were going to be robbed. The driver of the van requested the cashier allow the van to remain there four or five days, and paid fifteen days in advance. However, the night of July 16, the van had gone, and it did not return. After the explosion and the public notice that a white Trafic van had been involved, they contacted the police. They had noticed, too, that the van looked to be carrying a considerable weight: the body appeared to have dropped lower than its normal height. They recalled that the person who paid the ticket spoke in Spanish, with a provincial Argentine accent.

Again, it seemed there was something more happening here. Was the driver a member of the local connection, or somebody who had infiltrated the group; and, in the latter case, had the terrorists grown suspicious of him, and determined finally to remove the van from where he had left it? Who was the Argentine who had repaired and parked the van? And, why park the van with another car behind?

In the second volume, I learned of an insurance inspector who had taken several photos of the burned van that was later to be purchased by Carlos Telleldin. Those photos had never been requested, even though they would have helped to identify the original body of the van. The same thing happened with the van's plates: nobody had contacted the Department of Transit to determine whether some traffic infraction had been recorded in the days leading up to the explosion. I was not an investigator, but I felt, after a few hours of reading, that the clearest thing lacking in the case was simple common sense. There were several survivors who might have given some details on the driver, the van, or circumstances related to the explosion, yet after more than three years the majority had never been called to give testimony. On the other hand, some of the clues were clearly leading nowhere from the beginning. Nonetheless, Galeano had continued those lines of investigation with a stubbornness that should have suggested a more certain course. I was perplexed.

Our index and database grew at an unstoppable rate; after a month of reading I was able to present my first request for additional measures. I recall when I read the first draft of my request, I was somehow ashamed of having to instruct the tribunal to perform some elementary task, such as to interrogate a witness or clear person of interest who had not yet been questioned.

As my reading advanced, new and unexamined evidence began to arise. In volume ten, when asked whether they had noticed anything suspicious prior to the attack, numerous witnesses recalled that a helicopter flew over the AMIA building several times the night before the explosion, in what seemed to be a search of the area—yet Galeano never inquired as to the identity of the pilot or the purpose of his flight. A vehicular spring, which had lodged in the spine of the man in charge of the building across the street from AMIA, belonged to a model larger than the van presumed to have exploded. After some research, I discovered that those springs—distinct from those provided by Renault—had served as a suspension for the rear end of the Trafic van. Accordingly, it seemed somebody had reinforced the van to support the additional weight of the explosive device: TNT alone can weigh between twelve and fourteen hundred pounds, in addition to the several hundred pounds of dirt. This was further evidence against Telleldin, who was supposed to have done some mechanical work on the van prior to its sale. I was excited, and typed up this new evidence, along with some additional information collected from my readings for my first presentation to the court.

Whenever attorneys submit a paper to the courts, custom obliges us to include some formality—such as the Americans' "your Honor," or "as your Honor pleases". In our written proceeding, we typically conclude any submission to a judge with the phrase, *Será justicia:* "There will be justice." There are no written rules on the subject, but it is an age-old custom. In Memoria Activa, we altered the phrase, and it always produced a funny feeling to submit a request to Galeano that included the Biblical quotation *Justicia, justicia perseguirás* (Deut 16:20), "Justice, justice shall you pursue," added to the bottom. A small thing indeed, but it served as a constant reminder for Galeano that we were after him.

7

COLLATERAL DAMAGE

Argentina is a strange case in world history. One of the five most important countries at the beginning of the 20th century, with a highly-educated population and several Nobel Prize winners to its name, by the 1990's the nation had changed: the government was failing, and could not inspire its forces or its citizens to any meaningful unity, even following the bombing of the Israeli Embassy. Despite the number of people working with the judge, despite the Federal Police and the secret services, and the *División Unidad Antiterrorista* (DUIA) in particular, despite the Excalibur software and all the technology at hand, the investigation had stalled. After three years, we knew only what we had learned in the first days of the investigation. To be certain, my countrymen were corrupt, but they were not inefficient. My only way to reach the center of the web of cover-ups was to expose it to the public and the press. This would happen in its own manner, I was certain, with the passing of time.

Every measure that simple common sense suggested was systematically refused, and the investigation was lost in an accumulation of irrelevant data, amassing stacks of written paper only to demonstrate the tribunal's efforts, and Galeano's industriousness. At the time, this behavior was beyond my comprehension. Reading the results of three years of supposed work, I arrived at the only possible conclusion: such sloppy work was entirely purposeful. I was furious. This was the single greatest massacre in Argentina's history, apart from the lengthy crimes under the dictatorship, yet nobody seemed to care.

I arranged a meeting in my offices with the President of AMIA in order to ask him if he knew how the investigation was going, if he was aware of his counselors' inefficiency. The meeting was brief, and he affirmed his support of his counselors and the official investigation. Such a response from so prominent a figure in the Jewish community puzzled me.

I was not naive and it was already clear for me that Galeano was covering up something. I was intrigued, however, as to how the other private prosecution team of AMIA and DAIA could support Galeano's work and his official story. They had been victims of the explosion, and beyond that, both concrete institutions represented another group of victims as well as the families of the victims, too. How could they consent to such a scandal?

In that time, I wasn't able to understand that apparent contradiction. Beatriz Gurevich, an Argentine sociologist who studied the behavior of the Jewish institutions at the AMIA case wrote:

> "(O)nly a few people at the core of AMIA and DAIA had real knowledge of what was going on with the investigation; few knew the role of the government in the cover-up. The victims' families were not informed... Not asking questions and having faith (more than trust) became a symbol of communitarian spirit and reciprocal solidarity." (GUREVICH, B., " Passion, Politics and Identity: Jewish Women in the Wake of the AMIA Bombing in Argentina," The Hadassah-Brandeis Institute, 2005)

Memoria Activa was the dissenting voice and issued denunciations about the cover-up and about the inefficiency of the judge in charge of the investigation. According to Gurevich, we were *"perceived as an intrusion into the field of DAIA's incumbencies."* Although I respect some of her conclusions, I disagree with her explanations concerning the behavior of AMIA and DAIA in the judicial proceeding. She described them as being incapable of making a diagnosis about the pace of the preliminary judicial investigation which contributed to the veiling of intentional deviations by Galeano. I see the conclusion as too simple. In my opinion, the truth behind it is more complex and sordid, and requires a look into the political environment surrounding the attack. I wasn't able to see it then, but many years later, writing an article for the Southwestern Journal of International Law, the truth finally appeared in the form of interchanging dates and meetings and documents.

Following the Madrid Conference, talks between Israeli and Syrian delegations commenced in Washington under the framework of the Madrid formula. During 1994, negotiations were held on the ambassadorial level in Washington. In July 1994 the terrorist attack on AMIA happened, exactly in the middle of these talks. The attack led to focused discussions on security arrangements and the convening of two meetings between the Israeli and Syrian chiefs-of-staff in December 1994 and June 1995.

The day after the bomb, a declassified cable from the Argentine Ambassador in Israel to the Argentine government states: *"For the Israeli government it is important to coordinate with our version of the attack coincidentally - mainly by its impact we will have a way to present the issue to direct Israeli public opinion - given that opposition parties and some media are using the fact to attack harshly government peace policy of Rabin."*

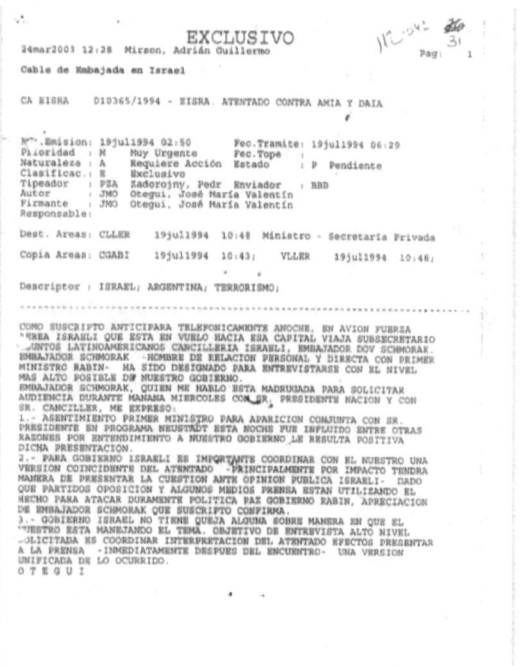

Copy of the cable from Argentine Ambassador in Israel about the trip of Dov Schmorak

In the early morning of July 19, 1994 Argentine Ambassador to Israel Otegui cabled the Argentine Foreign Ministry, informing them that former Israeli Ambassador to Argentina Dov Schmorak was flying to Buenos Aires as special envoy from Prime Minister Rabin, with the mission to meet Menem and coordinate the version that will be announced to the world. After meeting Menem, Schmorak declared to the press: *"Possibly, the number one on the list of suspects is Iran. There are Islamic fundamentalist organizations inspired by Iran, financed by Iran, trained by Iran, but not Iranian, like Hezbollah, in Lebanon."*

On September 27, 1994, a private meeting took place at the United Nations in New York, between President Menem and Foreign Minister Peres where the AMIA attack was considered.

Later that year, President Menem visited Syria, presumably trying to broach both the Israeli and Syrian positions.

The terrorist attack was not sponsored by these Arab nations, but most probably it had been performed by Hezbollah alone. To blame any of these nations for supporting the attack would be an unbeatable setback to the peace negotiations. The necessary conclusion was that Israel was not interested in blaming any of its new partners for the AMIA bombing, and this was the instruction sent from Israel to the main Jewish institutions in Argentina. What had been done had been done already and nobody can reverse the clock. Collateral damage.

The AMIA and DAIA leadership knew of the cover up, and they were instructed to support the inefficient work of Galeano that was clearly going nowhere, as well as the incredible waste of time and efforts in an investigation that has no more substance than an eggshell. They followed those principles of knowledge, surveillance, and discipline mentioned by Gurevich. The problem was that the investigation was so poor, so inefficient, so incredibly clumsy, that it was unsustainable to defend that conglomerate of feeble evidences collected by Galeano. I can only imagine the struggle of the leaders of the Jewish institutions to try to make palatable what was clearly impossible to digest. I have no sorrow for them. They were arrogant and incredibly blind obliging their representatives to believe the "official story." In spite of its gaps, shadows and absurdities, they were convinced that it was going to be accepted by public opinion. The situation could have been hilarious if we could forget the horror of the tragedy they were hiding.

But back in 1998, I didn't have all these explanations. Later that year, in New York, I met with members of the World Jewish Council, a representative of the Simon Wiesenthal Center –the same organization that originated my first contact with Memoria Activa - and other prominent members of the American Jewish community, and all left me with the same feeling. I explained the investigative gaps, I presented them a list of the investigators' inexplicable mistakes, the lost evidence and the miscarriages of justice on the part of the tribunal, and yet it was clear they hadn't believed me. After all, Beraja was Vice-President of the World Jewish Council. What had this gentile, who emerged from out of the blue, been insinuating? Did this guy mean to accuse the Argentine Jewish community of collaborating with a government cover-up? Nobody believed me. Did my work suffer because I was a gentile? I wondered if the Jewish community held any animosity toward me. It was a strange situation: on the one hand, I had always been fascinated with World War II, a kind of paroxysm of evil; with the feverish personality of an obscure Austrian corporal who galvanized a country at his back; with people torturing and killing others simply for being Jewish, or homosexual, or Gypsy. On the other hand, I had begun to feel strangely as though I were a part of it; as though, simply because I was a human being, I too had faced those atrocities. I lived in Germany for six long years; I studied there, I loved there, I mastered the language and I felt, and I still feel, that a part of me was indeed German, in spite of my family name and my ancestors from Italy, France, and Spain. I felt good being there, I obtained my PhD there, I even wrote a book in German, on the Malvinas (Falklands) War. Was it because I somehow understood the Germans that I was fascinated with the depravity of that generation? Of course, my German friends and colleagues had nothing to do with War World II. We were born years afterward. I had grown accustomed, visiting friends' homes, to encountering photographs of their fathers and grandfathers in uniform from the German forces during the war hanging on the walls. Everybody had been at war! That doubled my fascination; it was unbelievable to me that the nation that had produced Wagner, Schubert, Goethe, Dürer, Hesse, and Brahms, had also produced Himmler and Eichmann, Auschwitz, Dachau, Bergen Belsen, and the rest. What was the part of their DNA that produced these contradictions? I read *Mein Kampf* with fascinated horror, and I realized everything was there. I could underline the premonitory paragraphs, read with the clairvoyance of the future reader all that was going to happen, without surprise, later on. Who could really be unaware of what happened? And that book had been written in 1923, twelve years before the Arian Laws were passed, fifteen years before the Kristallnacht. Why didn't these people listen? Are all destined to be deaf to reality? Didn't the same things recur in Argentina thirty years later, when we learned every day of new disappearances? Who could be surprised if you had fed the monster and let it grow until it was too late to stop it?

In a way, my thoughts on the matter were contradictory. I had participated bravely in a fight against injustice, or at least I thought I had; but in reality, I had a considerably greater battle to wage against my own demons, against cowardice, against complacency and inaction. A human being is such a mystery. How can you turn away?

Shortly after meeting with the members of the World Jewish Council in New York, I agreed to meet the father of a victim of the Israeli Embassy bombing. I received him at the Yale Club where I was lodged. He begged me to take the Embassy case; he wanted justice for his son. Regretfully, I explained that a second case was beyond my capacity, overloaded as I was with the AMIA investigation. Years later, I would regret that decision, when we uncovered the AMIA bombing cover-up. Memoria Activa had not been engaged with the Embassy bombing, and because nobody had been pushing its investigation, that case had wound up in the borrowers of one judicial office. After meeting with the Jewish community abroad, it was clear we were going to work alone.

The blast in AMIA opened two different lines of investigation: on the one hand, the planners and executors of the bombing belonged to a foreign anti-Semitic terrorist group, with probable connections to the Islamic Jihad and Hezbollah located in Syria, Lebanon, or Iran. This was the international connection. On the other hand, investigators were exploring the local connection: the local group that had supplied the terrorists with the means to transport the bomb. The international connection was clearly out of my reach, unless the written proceeding brought some new information to light. My concern would be the local connection, the only line of inquiry I could control.

After reading all the files I received, I challenged myself to develop a logical syllogism, a reasoning based on a premise collected from my initial conclusions, something I should accept before proceeding. I had to accept that a van had been used to attack AMIA, and the engine that was discovered did in fact belong to Carlos Telleldin. This postulate left out all possible theories that the bomb had already been at AMIA, or had been placed in the trash container, or had been carried by the Bolivian workers or anybody else with access to the building. In addition to the few pieces of the van recovered at the blast site, a shock absorber from the van had also been projected into the spinal cord of the porter at the building across the street. It had been lodged with such pressure between the man's vertebrae, the coroners could only remove it by snapping the bones of the spine. This was a macabre discovery, but it cleared any doubt over the existence of the van.

When I confronted Galeano about the helicopter flight, he told me that the listed helicopter belonged to the Federal Police. I recall that I looked at him, expecting more. But he said nothing.

What were the police searching for? My only answer is that they were searching for the bomb or the van. Which might mean a high-ranking member of government intelligence—most probably a member of the secret services—had been in contact with a terrorist member or else infiltrated their group, and learned about their objective. For unknown reasons, it seems they lost contact with the terrorists, though they knew the AMIA building was the target. The conclusions deduced from this presumption were overwhelming: if the secret services knew AMIA was in danger, they should have increased measures to prevent the attack: prohibited access to the building, evacuated the street, anything to prevent such a loss of human lives. Perhaps they didn't know anything with certainty, but they should have taken measures nonetheless. How can their inaction be explained? You must recall that two years prior to the AMIA bombing, the Israel Embassy had been similarly destroyed, in the first foreign terror attack on Argentina soil. That happened in 1992, under Menem's government. Perhaps the embarrassment of that incident inspired the Argentine secret services to seek redemption in discovering a major terrorist cell within the country. Perhaps they had a plan to dissolve this cell, yet by unknown means the terrorist in turn discovered the trap. Following this line of reasoning, I arrived at a more far-flung realization: if the Argentine secret services knew anything at all concerning an attack against an Israeli objective, then surely the Mossad, the Israeli intelligence service, must have known it as well.

In accordance with the mentioned coordination between the Argentine and Israeli governments, the feeble Iranian theory began to take form in the proceedings.

In August 1994, Galeano flew in the Presidential plane Tango 04 to Venezuela to interview a supposedly Iranian repentant, Manoucher Moatamer. When he returned, immediately after getting off the plane, he was interview by several reporters, and Galeano pronounced a phrase that will be remembered for ever: "you are going to fall on your back." Then, surprising even the journalists that were interviewing him, Galeano finished the meeting with the reporters and went to the Presidential house in Olivos to inform President Menem. There, presumably, he projected a videotape of the interview with Moatamer. Beyond the fact that a Federal Judge, who, in theory at least, should be independent from any other power, wanted to see the President and inform him, deserves some critical comments. The promise that the reporters will "fall on their back" remained clearly unfulfilled. Something changed during that interview with the Executive, at least, concerning Galeano's public exposure.

When in September 2017 Israeli Prime Minister Benjamin Netanyahu visited Argentina, he reaffirmed what had been always the official story: *"We know without a doubt that Iran and Hezbollah initiated and backed up the attacks."*

In the name of God, what was going on here? Were we in the middle of an international fight between secret services? I have no doubt that if the Mossad or the Argentine secret services had taken any preventative measures, the results would have been quite different. But it happened. Somehow, something went wrong, and the bomb detonated. Should we accept then that AMIA was "collateral damage"? Was this the final answer to my questions?

Finally, at the end of August 1997, two months after receiving the first two hundred seventy volumes of the case, I submitted my first written request to the tribunal, proposing several new measures for collecting evidence. The request, I thought, was respectfully written: I began by stating that it was my obligation to collaborate with the investigation, and that I only wanted to produce some results in the case. The irony was unavoidable. I requested evidence that should have already been obtained in the three years since the investigation began. Certain of my requests were so obvious, there was no way to avoid seeming to criticize the inaction of the court. I was certain to maintain a respectful tone nonetheless. Later on, we would have reason enough for combat.

The request was divided in sections, pertaining to the different lines of the investigation. In each section, I proposed a number of additional measures to procure needed evidence. The first section was dedicated to the explosion in the AMIA building, proposing to call several witnesses who, as of my request, had yet to appear before the tribunal. All had survived or else witnessed the explosion. Galeano, after "exhausting" his means to locate certain of these witnesses, had ordered the police to begin an official inquiry on their whereabouts. That meant, in case any one of these people for any reason met with the police or any other national authority, a bulletin circulating the stations and offices would serve as a detaining order. A somewhat dramatic solution perhaps, but necessary nonetheless in order to collect all possible testimonies. My first list included eight potential witnesses who hadn't been called by the tribunal, two of whom already had inquiries posted on their whereabouts, whose addresses we found in the Buenos Aires telephone directory. I do not mean to suggest our exceeding cleverness. It was an elementary conclusion: in 1997, cell phones and beepers had just begun to appear, and the most common connection we had were the landline telephones. It was mere common sense. At the least, a federal judge in Galeano's position should be certain he's truly exhausted all the resources available to him before issuing an order to the police. Three years after the bomb, and the tribunal still had not performed an elementary search for witnesses; they had merely issued an order for detention.

The second section of my request concerned the blast itself. Reading the testimonies of witnesses who had already spoken before Galeano, I discovered two important facts: the first was the existence of another car, not recorded at the proceeding, one of the several parked in front of the AMIA building. These cars were mostly destroyed in the explosion. However, by crosschecking several different testimonies, I learned that the owner of one car in particular, which had not been so badly damaged, simply drove off after the blast. Yet nobody in the previous three years had paid any attention to it. I was able to interconnect a couple of witnesses, who provided the name of the car owner. There was a motorbike, too, whose owner never had testified, listed among the vehicles damaged by the blast. Perhaps both testimonies would prove irrelevant, but it was elementary to exhaust the list of people who, being present at the time of the explosion, might have observed something.

Another point I underlined in my request was the fact that the patrol car parked in front of the building had no battery, an issue which was not new. One of the policemen had phoned the precinct from within the AMIA building itself, requesting help in removing the battery and replacing it later that morning. Yet the question remains: what was the logic in leaving an immobile patrol car to protect the AMIA building? I suppose it was the cold which that morning convinced the officers to seek a replacement battery in order to use the heating—but the car had been sitting there, dead, several days beforehand. This was something that required further investigation.

Another section concerned the van. It was clear from reading documents and testimonies that Telleldin and his wife were equally liable. Ana had been present when the engine was stripped from the original burned van, and she carried this engine in her car to a second workshop, where it was installed in the final body of the van finally used in the attack. Nevertheless, only Telleldin had been detained, and Ana was still free. My request to detain Ana Boragni was refused by one of Galeano's *"téngase presente"* decisions—equivalent to being ignored. It was preposterous. I didn't know whether Telleldin or his wife were actively involved with the attack, but I was convinced they at least knew the identity of the last owner of the van, and Galeano's refusal was equivalent to concealing of the local connection. Galeano's reluctance to investigate Ana suggested an arrangement between Galeano and Telleldin, or else between Galeano and a superior, ordering him to leave Telleldin alone. After three years of second-rate investigation, such a situation was unacceptable—but it seemed we in Memoria Activa were the only ones upset. The videotape scandal confirmed an accord between Galeano and Telleldin. Telleldin, producing several contradictory testimonies throughout the proceeding, covering the few bits of truth with an overwhelming number of lies, preferred to remain in prison rather than incriminate the original local connection. A prison in Argentina, cramped and overcrowded, might be likened to an antechamber of hell. During my time working in San Isidro, I was obliged as clerk of the court to visit the main prison establishments in the province every month. The experience was depressing. Overcrowded prisons, many of them exceeding three times their capacity, were transformed into schools of delinquency, where rapes were a daily occurrence, and the only activity was to walk in circles around the yard, hundreds at a time, most of them planning their future criminal activities. The smell of urine, cooking, sweat and human grease stained the visitor's clothes. Telleldin preferred eight years in this godforsaken place to the risk of informing. Of course, it should be noted that his situation had been improved by the strange doings of power: he shared his lodgings with the VIP inmates, such as an Italian mafia boss awaiting extradition, or a famous Argentine guerrilla member. He occupied not a cell block, but a small house on the ground floor of Villa Devoto, with his own kitchen and yard, isolated from the other inmates. In his free time, which was plentiful, he completed a correspondence course and obtained his law degree. Another inmate related to the AMIA case, Juan Jose Ribellí, the policeman who had been accused by Telleldin, also received his law degree from the same university. Yet even having these comforts, he was in prison nonetheless.

Regarding the sacks of dirt piled within the van, I proposed a chemical analysis of that soil to determine where it came from; if so, perhaps we could approximate the location of the bomb's initial preparation—or else, where the van itself had first been loaded. When this report finally arrived, we learned with dismay that the sample had been contaminated with foreign elements, and no accurate analysis could be presented. It was impossible to collect another sample, because Galeano had cleaned up the debris and dumped it in the river.

Another section of my request concerned Santa Rita, the firm which owned the container at the entrance of the AMIA building. Nassif Haddad, the owner of Santa Rita, was a Syrian ally of Menem, who himself had personal ties to Syria. Along with the lot for the storage of containers and the deposit of rubble, Haddad owned a quarry in the province, where he used explosives identical to those used in the AMIA attack. This could all be mere coincidence; but, surprisingly enough, even if during his testimony, Haddad asserted that neither he nor anyone from his firm had ever brought explosives to his offices in the city, a chemical inspection carried out on their premises found evidence of these very explosives. What's more, the final destination for the driver of the container parked at Pasteur was a vacant lot belonging to another Syrian, who had called Telleldin the week before the attack. These events deserved a deeper investigation. Yet all such requests on my part were refused by Galeano with a laconic "at the moment, *téngase presente.*" Such an answer from the judge three years into a stalled investigation was astonishing, but I would grow accustomed to his parsimonious attitude in the time to come.

Something similar happened when I proposed to interrogate the staff of the 5th and 7th Police Precincts, who shared custody of the AMIA building. I requested that both precincts bring to the tribunal their official logbooks for that date, showing the distribution of shifts covering AMIA. Three years after the blast, this had not been done before. After three years of investigation, the investigating judge had yet to consider speaking with the people who watched over the AMIA building day and night. I wanted to know why they left a patrol car sitting without a functioning battery on the day of the attack. I wanted to know whether they had seen anything in the days and nights leading up to the attack, anything they might have recalled after the bombing. Finally, the tribunal agreed to gather and question the policemen from those precincts, but I received their statements with dismay: each one was identical, as though they had copied the same text until they knew it by heart. I spoke with one of Galeano's clerks, who had been in charge of interrogations. The clerk of the court in Argentina must be an attorney and act as a kind of notary giving faith to any act the judge had done. He had received more than fifty identical statements, and he was not surprised. When I said it was unacceptable, the declarations were useless because the policemen hadn't been asked anything of importance, the clerk of the court only grinned and responded: "Don't worry, Alberto. We will call them again." Yes, they would call them again and again, fill a few volumes in order to prove their activity, but not one of the testimonies would clarify anything. What better results can you expect of investigators who don't care about their work? That day was crucial for me, because I finally understood, was finally convinced that no matter how clear the evidence became, the investigation would only ever be a facade. They had decided it in advance: the AMIA case was not going anywhere. When the log books finally arrived, several years later, it was clear they had been tampered with; the original entries were deleted and overwritten, but even that work was so poor you could see the erasures and markings on the page. When I notified the tribunal of the tampering, Galeano's clerk said that if I wanted to make a criminal complaint, I was free to do so. It was ludicrous. Any public official made aware of a criminal act had the legal duty to report it.

In my first request, I appealed for several other measures concerning testimonies dispersed throughout several volumes, but I would like to recall one request in particular that has not been clarified to this day. While reading volume twenty-five, I learned that in October of 1994, two months after the attack, a Lebanese man named Ali Chehade Al Hassan was detained during a random inspection in a warehouse, where he was illegally rerouting electricity from a neighboring building. Another coincidence? Just checking illegal connections with a judge? This was really weird. During his arrest, the police discovered four pounds of TNT, originally packaged by the United State military. Trotyl had been used to detonate the amonal within the AMIA building, the same explosive fertilizer used in the Oklahoma City bombing of 1995. Al Hassan also had in his possession falsified credentials as military attaché for the Syrian Embassy in Argentina **and** pamphlets concerning the Syrian National Socialist Movement. He was living on a property belonging to an Argentine citizen of Syrian origin, and when a house seizure was ordered against the owner, authorities discovered and seized a shield of the Syrian army, various propaganda related to the Palestinian struggle, and videotapes concerning Hezbollah and the war in Lebanon, among other materials. Had I by chance discovered the international connection? In any case, the evidence collected against Al Hassan was by far more important than Galeano's presumptions that the Iranian Embassy in Argentina had assisted the attack. The only link suggestion the connection of Iranian diplomats was the statement of the lone Iranian "repentant," who had supposedly worked with the Iranian secret services in Venezuela. The repentant provided, at best, a confused explanation of supposed links between the Iranian Embassy and Hezbollah. Among the materials Galeano had gathered was a suggestive photo of Moshe Rabbani, an Iranian religious leader, at a Buenos Aires mosque, taken by the Argentine secret services in December of 1993, eight months before the AMIA bombing, looking for a Renault Trafic van. Galeano had never called Rabbani for interrogation. The strangest part of the story was that the Iranian diplomats were still in Argentina, untouched. "They were diplomatically immune," Galeano told me. "Wrong," I said. "They might have become immune the day the Iranian Government informed you of their protection under diplomatic immunity, but before that moment, they were not." That was one of my favorite subjects as a teacher of international law, and I brought Galeano several juridical articles I had published in Argentina concerning diplomatic immunity. Even so, Galeano never called them in, and after several months, by which time they had already left Argentina, he sent a request to Interpol issuing a "Red Notice," which would have consequences later on, when one of the diplomats was located in London and the British tribunals refused to extradite him for lack of evidence. Rabbani's situation was suspicious; when Galeano's investigation turned to Iran, he was appointed a diplomatic member of the Iranian Embassy—thus, immunized. In any case, the matter deserved investigation, but, as anybody with legal experience can see, evidence of an Iranian plot was not overwhelming.

I can't say the key to the AMIA case was Al Hassan, but I am certain he should have been investigated more thoroughly. Yet nothing was done against him. The next reference to him in the case files comes in a statement from the counselor of his cell inmate, who claimed Al Hassan had requested that he bring a message to some companions in Ciudad del Este, in Paraguay. When I learned that Al Hassan was free and his whereabouts unknown, it was clear Galeano didn't want to investigate the Syrian connection for fear of provoking certain friends of President Menem. Several years later, Galeano sent a police commission to Paraguay to locate and interrogate Al Hassan's former cellmate, who had also disappeared.

I never suspected that in discovering Al Hassan, I had uncovered the international connection of the AMIA case; but as I've said, his whereabouts should have been investigated more thoroughly. Where did he get the explosives? Why did he possess fake credentials for the Syrian Embassy? Why did he own propaganda from Hezbollah? Galeano ordered an investigation into the matter only after my request, entrusting the case to the DUIA—but nothing would ever come of their investigation.

. . .

That was the first written request I presented to Galeano. In the coming months, I would follow this with more than twenty additional requests, each containing approximately fifteen different measures to be performed by the tribunal. Some of these could be subdivided into dozens of sub-measures for the collection of evidence. The final tally amounted to more than four hundred new measures of investigation. That was accomplished simply by reading the case files. One thing was clear after I submitted my requests: it didn't matter what evidence I sought or the type of measure I requested; somebody high in the government had decided the AMIA case would come to nothing, and he or she—or they—had secured the compliance of Galeano, the prosecutors, and all others involved.

Something else was clear: by pressuring the tribunal to pursue more solid evidence, I would make many enemies, and, more importantly, I would be subject to the scrutiny of the secret services. I was certain all my phones were tapped. Every time we met with Memoria Activa, we immediately removed the batteries from our cell phones, so as to prevent their use as microphones for the secret services. If possible, our meetings took place outdoors. I recall meeting a critical opposition leader who was interested in the AMIA case, on a bench in a park near my office. Those were times of persecution and paranoia.

By 1999, I was convinced that even if I could bring the perpetrators of the attack directly to Galeano, he would do nothing. Having crashed again and again against a wall of incomprehension, it seemed the AMIA case would be buried, just like the Embassy bombing before it.

Then, we went to the press.

There was a press office in the lobby of the very building where Galeano's tribunal was located, and I began to offer weekly - then, daily - interviews. The prosecutors and I were invited, along with the representatives of Memoria Activa, onto several talk shows, where we expressly denounced the cover-up. We presented the incredible number of documents proving the inefficiency of the investigation so far. We went to the Jewish newspapers and programs, to all journals, and TV shows, to the radio, and then to the major newspapers around the world. We gave interviews to The New York Times, the Economist, Time, Newsweek, and the major European press. The cover-up would be exposed worldwide.

Going to the press

When our comments on the failure of the investigation began to appear in print, Galeano's attitude toward us changed accordingly. We were effectively ruining the performance he had been free to direct within the security of the mysterious lines of investigation and the support of the government. We were disrupting the peaceful intermission between the anniversaries of the attack, when once a year he would have to come up with something to placate the public. Thus, a new line of investigation was to be followed, or an arrest would be made, or a trip to France or Switzerland would be undertaken, presumably in the pursuit of new evidence.

Galeano decided to apply the statute of limitations to Telleldin, and set him free. I met with Galeano around that time, and we finished our meeting in a very bad way. *"What do you know about the statute of limitations?"* he barked at me. *"I will show you what I know!"* I responded on my way out the door.

I went to the offices of the Argentine Bar Association, located in the basement of the court's building. I furiously typed my request that the Chamber of Appeals reverse Galeano's decision to free Telleldin. After submitting the appeal, on the way back to my office, I received a call from Luis Dobniewsky, DAIA's attorney, begging me to attend a meeting in his office nearby. I was reluctant, but it was the first time a private prosecutor for either of the two institutions had requested a meeting. When I arrived, the attorneys from DAIA were there already, along with Dobniewsky's partners and several other attorneys for AMIA and DAIA. "Your appeal does not comply with the formal requirements of the new procedural code," said Dobniewsky's partner, Javier Astigarraga, a red-haired attorney with a Basque name. "Of course it does," I responded. I was well aware of the new procedures. Before these changes, you could appeal without particular explanation. Now, such appeals needed to be concrete, at the least clarifying the disputed issues. My request was austere, but it complied with all the new requirements. After they insisted again that it wasn't enough, Astigarraga stood up, went to a side room, and returned with a faxed copy of my request. I was astonished. The request had been presented to the tribunal less than an hour before. Their only source could have been the tribunal itself. They were not only working with Galeano, but Galeano was providing them whatever documents I presented—while I in turn received month-old copies, and those only scarcely. I questioned the ethics of the clear favoritism the tribunal was expressing towards them, and left the meeting. In the end, we won the appeal; Telleldin remained in jail until the end of the proceeding. But I learned my lesson that day: I would need to identify my true allies, as well as my foes.

8

THE FINAL DROP

What, then, was the drop that made the cup run over? What changed my attitude so radically and finally exhausted my patience? Looking back, I believe the aforesaid conversation with Galeano was the final straw. I was strongly opposed to Galeano's decision. It would be a victory for Telleldin, and would only encourage his lies.

Until that moment, I had been somehow reluctant to believe that AMIA and DAIA, Menem and his government and the Argentine justice system itself had no interest in the truth, not even in pursuing the local connection to the case despite the considerable evidence to think otherwise. As I have explained, it will be only many years later when I will confirm my worst fears. Perhaps my attitude was simply a consequence of my admitted ignorance or naivety of political matters. The AMIA case demanded a certain understanding of the political environment, not an interest in justice alone. In a search for the truth, such an examination of the evidence would of course be meaningful. Yet, in order to understand Argentina's actions (and inactions), events must be analyzed from another perspective.

The first premise of a logical syllogism might be that the

government must have been hiding something significant to so greatly impede a rational investigation. Ironically, the cover-up itself was so clumsy, they revealed an incredible number of their own omissions and mistakes. Perhaps they thought they could never be discovered.

A second premise might be added: we must presume that nobody within Argentine political circles wished the AMIA bombing to occur, and that the sorrow they expressed was real; but, having been ultimately unable to stop the attack, in part owing to their own negligence and incompetence, Menem's government sought primarily to circumscribe the damage done and minimize political consequences. Typically, the nation's security policy would be questioned, and a serious investigative commission or independent prosecutor would be contracted to determine what had happened.

It seemed, however, that SIDE might have been connected with the event from the very beginning. Three circumstances suggested as much: the unexplained flight of the helicopter the night before the explosion; the inexplicable and simultaneous disappearance of sixty tapes documenting Telleldin's earliest interrogations from the offices of both the Federal Police and SIDE; and, lastly, the address book seized from Telleldin during his arrest, from which several names and telephone numbers had been cut out, along with his electronic agenda, which was returned to him only after its contents were erased. Telleldin's silence and lies, too, pointed to a cover-up. I suspected that SIDE had infiltrated the terrorist cell, obtained the van from Telleldin, and then, for unknown reasons, had let the terrorists go free.

Telleldin was jailed for his role in the attack, but his sole link to the bombing was as the last registered owner of the van. We might also add his knowledge of who had purchased the van from him. He was protecting somebody, that much was certain. At the beginning, I thought perhaps a member of his family had been his connection with the terrorist group, and for his or her sake he would not confess the truth. But that was not enough. Telleldin was incarcerated then for more than five years without offering a single clue. Every member of his family had been incriminated at some time or another, and I did not buy the idea that he was so anxious to protect them, fulfilling some kind of unknown mafia rule. No, the cover-up must have been for the sake of somebody far more important. Perhaps some person or group that had assisted or allowed his illegal activities purchased the van—a person or group so powerful, Telleldin preferred eight years in prison to the danger of confession. SIDE was an obvious candidate for such a group.

Rather than accept the consequences of its actions, SIDE closed ranks and aimed to present a united front. Handling its guilt in this way, and being generally unprepared to confront public derision, a cover-up appeared its only alternative. Unavoidable.

In order to understand this, one should recall that the Israeli Embassy bombing had already revealed SIDE's inability to prevent and manage such a catastrophe. Did Menem and his government think the AMIA bombing could be treated with the same duplicity and indifference? In fact, they had managed to curtail most criticism up to that incident. They might claim to have done everything necessary to aid the investigation; they provided the tribunal with the most advanced forensic and investigative tools. They multiplied Galeano's personnel tenfold, including the addition of a twenty-man special forces team, and freed him from all other cases in order to dedicate his efforts to the AMIA case alone. Galeano used these incredible resources to fill page upon page with nothing.

Galeano's behavior was not owing simply to incompetence or negligence, as it might have appeared. His was a willful decision to impede the investigation. He filled volume upon volume, but it only amounted to a facade of an investigation. Any nonsense was sufficient. More important was to fill these pages to show that something was happening, no matter how futile. Galeano was following instructions. The results were willful, not accidental. He refused every one of my requests to investigate further into the mysterious helicopter flight. He answered merely that the helicopter belonged to the Federal Police, and they were performing a regular patrol. He and his gang, including the prosecutors Muellen, Barbaccia, and Nisman, his assistants, and his clerks of the court, were determined to fail in their investigation.

During our conversation, I realized Galeano's decision to free Telleldin was the fulfillment of a prior agreement. Up to then, I had tried several times, despite my clients' wishes for a more expeditious tactic, to bring Galeano onto the correct path of investigation. If he so desired, he could have changed his attitude entirely, and simply studied the evidence before him. I simply refused to believe that a federal judge would willfully impede an investigation of the most abhorrent terrorist act in his nation's history. I preferred to believe he simply didn't realize he was wrong. He was a political product of the federal justice system closely intertwined with the Executive and its policies. Why were AMIA and DAIA—both the most important Jewish institutions in Argentina, both victims of the attack—aiding the official version of the case? Why did they not seem to care to know what had really happened - to search for the truth, to dig to it, to be willing to get covered with mud and dregs in that pursuit?

One of the major principles I have learned in my years as an attorney is to never underestimate one's opponents. If I attribute nonexistent merits to my opposition, at least my opponent's virtues will never surprise me. I would prefer to be proven wrong in thinking the opposing party a threat, rather than be surprised by his cleverness. If he fails repeatedly, I will see his failure and ineptitude as the exception rather than the rule. Following these useful ideas, I have also learned to understand that my opposite has seen the same things as me. If he didn't, all the better—but again, I will not be taken by surprise.

Yet it was difficult to uphold such principles in the AMIA case. Telleldin and the officers he accused were incarcerated; the latter, I believe, were corrupt, and so were likely accused by Telleldin in return for favors—but they had nothing to do with the bombing. Galeano preferred to follow clues without much promise, and so refused our own proposals, which we derived from the facts of the case.

During the summer of 1998, I made my first visit to Washington D. C. on behalf of Memoria Activa, to contact my friends in the Human Rights Watch and CEJIL, two nonprofit organizations with strong ties to Latin America. At the time, I was obsessed with the thought that SIDE was surveilling me, and worried they might appear at my offices with any excuse and seize my archives on the AMIA case—which, by then, contained a full index with abstracts of the main texts, and transcriptions of various documents. A strange burglary had already struck our offices: a portable computer was stolen. Since I began to openly criticize the official version of the attack, I began to hear (or imagine I heard) mysterious clicking noises on my telephone. It was the main evidence of the cover-up occurring with the government's acquiescence, if not its direct support. I brought those archives with me to Washington, copied onto several disks, and I deposited those disks in the safe box of CEJIL. As my writings to the tribunal became more critical, the differences between our prosecution and the official version of the case became increasingly evident, and the national press began to publish our comments in print.

In that first visit to the U.S. capital, I discussed with my friends at CEJIL the possibility of presenting a claim against Argentina before the Inter-American Commission of Human Rights located in Washington, one of the central autonomous organs of the Inter-American Pact of Human Rights. During these discussions, we agreed it would be extremely difficult to convince the Inter-American Commission that Argentina, the victim of a terrorist attack, had in fact been covering up the truth, impeding the investigation and the search for justice. I returned to Buenos Aires, intending to study the matter deeper.

Soon after my return to Buenos Aires, early in 1999, I received a visit from Jose Miguel Vivanco, a young Chilean attorney in charge of the Latin American department of the Human Rights Watch. We had first met as young lawyers studying human rights violations, both trying to gain a footing in our new profession. I recall later a dinner in 1994, in Benihana's in New York, together with Jose Miguel and several other friends, when each one of us was anticipating an imminent change in our professional lives. I was the Argentine candidate for the prosecutor's position at an ad hoc International Tribunal for Yugoslavia. José Miguel had had his own interview, for a position in the Latin American office of Human Rights Watch. In my case, that chance mobilized my life in a way that was unexpected. I was a successful lawyer in Buenos Aires, but happy to open myself to the possibility of being Prosecutor before the International Tribunal for Yugoslavia. However, after some months, the South African Richard Gladstone was elected to the position, but the opportunity alone was a clear turning point in my life.

Now José Miguel and I met in a coffee shop in front of my apartment in Buenos Aires, where we discussed the chances of holding Argentina liable for, at least, reckless disregard concerning the investigation of the AMIA bombing. I was determined to present my case to the Inter-American Commission, and I explained to him my strategy.

About that time, I had read David Goldhagen's book, *Hitler's Willing Executioners*. The book was particularly well-written, and proved beyond all doubt something I had learned during my years in Germany: the majority of the German people knew what had been happening to the Jews during World War II—or else, at the least, knew they were being removed from their homes and incarcerated in an unknown, distant location. In a way, the situation described by Goldhagen was very much like Argentina's in the 1970's, when the military dictatorship was kidnapping members of the opposition. The greatest merit of Goldhagen's book was his extensive research on the subject, and the manner in which he presented his evidence to the reader. He constructed his argument with a collection of documents and testimonies: page upon page of evidence was compiled to build his proof. Like hitting a nail again and again with irrefutable evidence, Goldhagen's investigation left little room for any interpretation other than his own. The book was so solid in its conclusion, two of the most important weeklies in Germany, *Die Zeit* and *Der Spiegel*, dedicated their front pages and cover articles to his subject for two consecutive weeks. This was the model I wished to use in presenting our case to the ICHR. I wished to compile the evidence I had been collecting on the Menem administration's cover-up in the same conclusive way.

I explained this idea to Jose Miguel: to present such an immense volume of evidence, rebuttal would be impossible. Jose Miguel put me in touch with the sister organization of CEJIL in Buenos Aires, the Centro de Estudios Legales y Sociales, or CELS. CELS was then presided by Emilio Mignone, one of the visitors I had received during the Schwammberger case, when I requested a number of materials for my affidavit. After that meeting with Jose Miguel and, afterward, with my clients at Memoria Activa, we had agreed to introduce the claim before the next anniversary of the bombing. Memoria Activa would have something important to say that day. I discussed the alternatives with Laura, Diana, and Norma, and they all agreed with this strategy.

A week later, I met Andrea Pochak of CELS at another coffee

shop, on the corner of Las Heras and Coronel Díaz, three blocks away from my apartment. Meeting in coffee shops was certainly not the best way of going about things, but I was anxious to ensure privacy during our conversations; I didn't want the SIDE to know my plan before I had presented it.

Andrea was a young Jewish lawyer working on several cases related to human rights violations, and had extensive experience with the Inter-American Commission. I explained my

Andrea Pochak

plan to Andrea. It was the first of several such meetings, concerning preparations to approach the Inter-American Commission. She instructed me mainly on the procedural aspects and the language required for making such an unusual claim viable. We worked especially on the requirement of exhaustion of local remedies for a claim that theoretically was in a current, not finished, proceeding. We affirmed that it was not necessary the wait until the end for showing the clear attitude of the government for concealing the truth.

After a month, we developed a workable draft I was to complete in Washington before presenting it to the Commission. Andrea was bewildered by Galeano's investigation, and her collaboration was essential in drawing up the text to be submitted internationally. I still recall when we parted at our final meeting, and Andrea told me: "Alberto, we have made a fine piece of work, but please do not expect that we are going to win the case." Yes, her meaning was clear. From the outside, the task was near impossible: to convince the Inter-American Commission of Human Rights that Argentina, the victim of two horrendous terrorist attacks, had been covering up the truth and impeding the investigation. However, our claim was strong. We did not care what was expected, nor what was logical. We would confront the Commission with facts— indisputable, irrefutable facts.

Along with the few members of Memoria Activa who were aware of our plans, we decided the claim must be submitted before the fifth anniversary of the bombing. That would offer time enough to prepare speeches for the gathering, where the content and significance of our claim would be publicly announced.

9

GOING INTERNATIONAL

I leaned my forehead on the window of the plane, hoping to find some sleep. A moment before, I had once again finished reading our claim against Argentina, which I was to submit when we landed in Washington, D.C. I was no longer concerned about the case itself, only that our claim be accepted. I worried over the loose ends, the lack of explanations, the disproportion of questions to answers. I had read the full case twice through, yet I couldn't answer my main concern over the cover-up: why? Why they were acting so? Who was protecting whom, and from what? Knowing Argentina was an easy terrorist target didn't bring any comfort. Had it only been revenge against President Menem, as the rumor went? Menem's former colleagues in the Arab world had criticized him: a former Muslim, he converted to Catholicism for fulfilling the requirement of the current Argentine constitution for being elected president; he repudiated his Arab roots and joined the international coalition against Iraq in the Desert Storm campaign: he sent two patrol boats of the Argentine Navy to watch over the entrance of the Ormuz Gulf.

I thought of Lebanon, of Syria, of Gaza, of Israel. Films,

photographs, the horrible sounds of bombs in a residential quarter, clouds of dust rising among the scattering crowds, a street littered with bodies in the aftermath of a car bombing—it all flashed through my imagination. Mourners and victims. Half-burned books soiled with blood in a demolished cafeteria. And the looks of passersby, their initial horror and incomprehension turning to hate, a passion for vengeance passed from father to son, and so on. Recalling events in the Middle East, visions of death and loathing I had seen once on the news reappeared before my eyes again. A mob of mourners passing a casket draped with a Palestinian flag overhead, shouts of abhorrence and the high-pitched cries of women in black dresses and veils; the unsteady but hurried transport of the coffin to the cemetery gates, followed by a serpentine column of black-dressed mourners. A catch-22 situation: hate beyond comprehension, handed down from generation to generation, followed by bloody rituals promising death and revenge. I saw children with Palestinian headbands waving their Kalashnikovs at the cameras, firing to the heavens. A choir of voices shouting: "God is great," like a litany. "God is Great." I saw fanatic religious terrorists, planning indiscriminate damage to the Jewish world. I saw members of the Mossad searching the earth for perpetrators, a never-ending history of vengeance and retaliation. Arabs preparing their next attack, Israelis trying to prevent them, menace, torture, fueling further retaliation. Arabs killing, Israelis killing; you could no longer discern between them, nor remember how it had begun.

My questions lingered, and I began placing events as though pieces in a game of chess. If SIDE was informed of the attempt, if they suspected a bomb would be placed, if they had infiltrated a terrorist group and had learned of its intentions, then the Israeli Mossad must have been informed. Or perhaps just the opposite: the Mossad had infiltrated the group, and later informed SIDE. In any case, it seemed unlikely that one of the most powerful intelligence agencies in the world could not have known whatever the Argentinians knew. Perhaps the undercover agent, from whichever agency, had been discovered; perhaps a turn in destiny had allowed the terrorists to lose their pursuers. Despite their imaginable panic, the service members must have been unsuccessful in their attempts to reconstruct the van's itinerary. Was it due to this failure that the helicopter flew over the AMIA building the night before the attack? Did this explain the disappearance of Telleldin's interrogation tapes? All of this in a nation at the end of the world, lost, dominated by corruption, inefficiency and ineptitude. Should we believe the Mossad had not been present in Buenos Aires, after what had happened with the Israeli Embassy? Should we accept that the bomb took the most important and efficient intelligence officers in the world by surprise? Had they believed they could track down the terrorists again, and merely failed? Was the explanation so simple?

Questions. The van had rear doors, and a sliding door on its left side. I wondered how they knew of the sliding door, narrowing the source of the vehicle among the local van thefts within a four-month period prior to the blast. I took my question to the Fire Department, where the remains of the van were being kept. I was dismayed when I saw what had been recovered. A couple of twisted wheel rims, shock absorbers, several twisted and burned pieces of metal, and an engine. That was all. And Galeano had ordered the rest of debris (including certain unidentified parts of the van) dumped into the river.

Six large plastic barrels loaded into the van must have contained ammonium nitrate and fuel; an additional small container must have been filled with trotyl and wired to the barrels. Ammonium nitrate is a synthetic fertilizer which can be obtained nearly anywhere; its explosive properties are devastating, as shown in the accidental explosion at the chemical plant in Oppau, Germany in 1921, where a gigantic crater took the place of the factory. Was the driver a suicide bomber, or had the detonation been produced by remote control? I imagined a suicide bomber driving the van, wearing an explosive vest and holding an electric detonator in his hand. Had he been told the detonation would be more powerful if he rocketed through the entryway and entered the building? Was the idea to demolish the whole building, rather than devastate the facade and part of the front offices? How did they know of the gap between the empty container and the sidewalk? How many times had the terrorist group passed in front of the building to study the area? Did they possess construction blueprints for the building? Was the provision of the blueprints the key to infiltrating the group? Did anyone check if copies of the blueprints had been requested at the Town Hall? Did a car accompany the van, to show it the way? Had anybody checked whether surveillance cameras captured any salvageable footage along Pasteur at the time of the blast? Was the cover-up intended most of all to hide the fact that the Mossad and SIDE were engaged with the terrorist group, apart from all possible retaliation that took place later? Might the embarrassment of such a revelation have justified the cover-up in their minds? Was this the answer to all I was searching?

On July 16, 1999, I submitted our claim to the Commission's offices on H Street, where I received a stamped copy with the time and date of the presentation. The Secretary of the Commission was Jorge Taiana, an Argentinian forced into exile during the dictatorship, who was bewildered by my claim. The AMIA case was well-known around the world as one of the most severe terrorist attacks against a Jewish community outside Israel; but, in general, nobody would have yet supposed that Argentina's authorities were attempting to impede the investigation. Two members of the Inter-American

Jorge Taiana (left) and Commissioner Richard Goldman (right)

Commission were also Jewish: Professor Robert Goldman and Dean Claudio Grossman, both from American University. I wondered whether they would be as difficult to convince as the representatives of the World Jewish Council I had met in New York.

The accusation against Argentina was grounded on a violation of the integrity and right to life of the victims of the attack. We stated that Argentina had failed in its duty of preventing, investigating, and then punishing the perpetrators of the attack; the investigation was a mere façade built up by Galeano, with the complicity of the Argentine government. We stated that the right to seek justice on behalf of the victims and their families had been violated in Galeano's obstruction of our investigation. They violated, too, the right to a fair judicial process against those responsible for the attack. We stated that the Argentine state had not carried out this investigation thoroughly, and that it had not done everything in its power to clarify events.

The OAS in Washington where our claim was submitted

Then we turned to the facts of the case, explaining that our knowledge of events surrounding the explosion, five years after the fact, were yet the same as it had been during the immediate aftermath. That is, on July 18, 1994, at 9:53 AM, a van loaded with ammonal or ammonium nitrate exploded at the AMIA building in downtown Buenos Aires, killing more than eighty people and injuring over three hundred. The explosion totally destroyed the six-story building, and damaged those adjacent. The discovery of an engine belonging to Telleldin among the rubble might be added to this scarce list of proven facts, but that was all. Nothing more could be obtained from an inept investigation, handled by a judge whose only objective seemed to be a cover-up of all possible liabilities.

We stated that Argentina had failed because it did not implement the measures necessary to prevent this attack, keeping in mind that the Israeli Embassy bombing had occurred only two years earlier. The ineffectual investigation of the Embassy attack, in fact, abetted the attack against AMIA. The second attack confirmed the inadequacy of Argentina's security system, as well as the failure of its intelligence services.

We pointed out that AMIA did not have appropriate security prior to the attack: the patrol car guarding the building contained a dead battery, and had remained in that condition for several days. It was useless: it was impossible to move it, much less use its radio. The officers' only means of communication was a walkie-talkie provided by AMIA. And when the bomb exploded, the two policemen were not in their assigned positions. One of them was having coffee in the bar in front of AMIA. The other was reading a newspaper inside the useless patrol car.

Then we referred to the events in Milan; Dos Santos' warnings were not duly considered. The Argentine vice-consul did not report his visit to the Secretary of Foreign Affairs until July 19, the day following the attack, claiming that Dos Santos had only just come forward. Due to the evidence against her, the vice-consul admitted she had disregarded it at the beginning, and had not even reported it to the State Intelligence Bureau of the Argentine Embassy in Rome.

We stated that Argentina had failed in its duty to properly investigate the attack. Even though a great number of resources had been mobilized, there was none or little progress in the investigation.

The next item was Galeano's loss and destruction of evidence, amounting to reckless disregard. We stated that in a complex case like this one, the only possible way to identify the perpetrators would be to gather all possible evidence as it arose. We pointed out that the rubble of the AMIA building, which surely included essential pieces of evidence, had been lost forever. It had all been gathered after the attack using hydraulic excavators, together with masonry, car parts, and even human remains, without any order whatsoever. This was then transported in dump trucks to an open tract of land, near the river and the domestic airport. Although this situation had been constantly denounced, and this material was theoretically under the custody of the Federal Police, it was plundered several times, and items were later sold as antiques or souvenirs at several locations around Buenos Aires. Finally, in May of 1997, Galeano gave the authorization to use this material as filling for a section of land along the riverbank. This formed the foundations for the *Parque de la Memoria*, to remember the many victims of the military dictatorship. It was a cruel irony that the construction of this park required the loss of evidence pertaining to one of the most severe terrorist tragedies in Argentine history.

Documents and materials seized in several raids, too, were lost forever: we mentioned the tapes, computer disks, and agendas seized from Carlos Telleldin in his arrest, which disappeared soon after and were never seen again—except for the agendas and address books, which were mutilated and useless. Thin rectangular windows were cut out of each page, removing names, addresses, and phone numbers of certain of Telleldin's associates, leaving each page like a strange comb with irregular teeth. There were considerable differences between the written records of the seizures and the elements that were later delivered to the tribunal for our inspection. It was evident that somebody high in SIDE had authorized such a mishandling of collected evidence.

We stated that in many cases, for unknown reasons, the tribunal did not seize certain key pieces of evidence; and even when it did, the seizure was partial or the material was ultimately returned to its owner without having been analyzed at all. There are several instances wherein our proposed measures were rejected, which might have meant an important advance in the search for the truth. For example, Telleldin's computer was not seized from his home, but some computer disks were collected. We are speaking of a time when computers were only just becoming popular; backups were not yet so common, people being accustomed to saving data directly to the computer's hard drive.

We listed examples of several essential clues that Galeano did not pursue. We requested the logbooks of the 5th and 7th Precincts of the Federal Police, in order to learn the shifts for supervision of the AMIA building. Galeano did not allow this measure, though we had presented contradictions in the testimonies of several officers concerning their shift schedule.

In the case of Ali Al Hassan, too, Galeano had failed. Several items were seized from Al Hassan that suggested his involvement in terrorist activities, such as the false credential of military attaché for the Syrian Embassy, propaganda of Hezbollah, and four pounds of Trotyl, the same explosive used as detonator of the amonal in the AMIA bombing.

The same happened with the helicopter, which several witnesses claimed to have observed the night before the blast.

We stated that the tribunal displayed negligence in its handling of many eyewitness accounts: for instance, the tribunal only requested that one particular witness help to prepare an identikit, three years after the explosion, which length of time would clearly have affected his accuracy. A witness who stood in the doorway of a building across the street was called nearly four years afterward. People within the AMIA building during the explosion had not once been interviewed until we requested their statements. Perhaps the most paradigmatic example was the case of the trash collector, who survived only because the force of the explosion threw him into the empty container at the door of AMIA; he was called in nearly seven months after the blast. Even a witness who had filmed the aftermath of the explosion was only called in because we insisted, four years after the fact. Supposedly, many of these witnesses were overlooked because the tribunal struggled to learn their whereabouts—yet we located them with a simple search through the telephone directory. Several people claiming indemnity for damages had never been called to testify. Several witnesses' statements were fruitless simply owing to the ineptitude of their interviewer. For example, only after we interrogated a policeman who had spoken twice before with the tribunal, we learned that he had seen a suspicious car with Uruguayan plates pass several times in front of the AMIA building. The manner in which the tribunal handled these testimonies was persuasive evidence of its ineptitude and inefficiency.

We denounced the government's obstruction of the investigation. We referenced the case of the National Direction of Migrations, which kept a register of travelers entering and exiting the country. The Direction informed Galeano that it was impossible to provide him a list of all foreigners who recently arrived because it did not have access to a computerized database, relying instead on a manual system of registration. Despite the inadequacy of this system, which was used until 1996, a manual search surely could have been organized. Nothing happened, though, and the information never arrived. Another instance of governmental obstruction occurred when the Federal Police alerted Monjo, the dealer who sold the van to Telleldin, of his future seizure and detention, allowing him to gather his possessions and escape.

Altogether, they allowed countless pieces of essential evidence to disappear: agendas, diskettes, tapes and computers. Even the government's award to anyone with workable information relating to the attack had never been shared with the public.

We presented several legal irregularities Galeano had carried out during the investigation. He had employed practices foreign to the Argentine legal system. However, beyond the inherent nullity that Galeano's actions brought to the case, he contributed nothing to the investigation. We denounced his negotiations with Carlos Telleldin. The public disclosure of the videotape of Galeano handling with Telleldin was evidence enough of the tribunal's lack of respect for the proceedings. What's more, because the tape had been stolen from the tribunal's own safe, the insecurity of the tribunal's standards should have been clear.

We denounced Galeano's obstruction of our own investigation, particularly his order that several investigative lines be opened in cases separate from the main proceeding. This was a clear violation of due process. Later, we would obtain an order from the Chamber of Appeals that Galeano incorporate all these annexes and parallel investigations into the main proceeding. In any case, Galeano's violation of due process didn't contribute any new information or evidence to the investigation.

One particular request, that I had introduced at the beginning of my work, composed of several different proposed measures, was never -materially- incorporated into the proceeding. This revealed a clear disinterest on the part of the tribunal in enforcing the procedural norms, as well as a certain incompetence and ineptitude regarding their ability to maintain a certain order within the proceedings.

We finally requested that the Inter-American Commission admit our claim against Argentina. Getting that registration number was paramount; it would mean the Commission had initially accepted our claim. We worried for a while that perhaps our claim would not be sufficiently convincing. Who could imagine a terrorized state would cover up an investigation to discover its own attackers?

Upon my return to Argentina, Memoria Activa appointed Pablo Jacoby, an expert in criminal procedural law who had previously defended Jorge Lanata, to join me on the case. I was skeptical at first, thinking Pablo was not going to read the entire case, which by now consisted of more than four hundred and seventy volumes. In addition, Pablo was known for his work in federal justice, and I worried he might be soft on Galeano, for whatever sympathies he might maintain. Soon enough, however, I recognized my mistake. Pablo was a brilliant attorney, a born fighter, and after an initial meeting with Galeano, he too was convinced of the cover-up. He was Jewish, his cousin was a prominent Rabbi, and he knew the inner workings of the Jewish community better than anybody. For the first time since beginning the case, I felt that I was not fighting alone.

Memoria Actica private prosecutors: Alberto L. Zuppi and Pablo Jacoby

We agreed to wait, to see what would happen. The ICHR would inform the Argentine government of our demands, and Argentina would have to answer to our accusations. When the press received copies of our presentation, they were as astonished as us; they would become a major ally to our efforts.

On December 1, 1999, the Argentine government responded.

When I finally read a copy of the text, my feelings were mixed. On the one hand, the response was so incredibly clumsy and inept that for the first time, after so many hours and hours of work, I realized that perhaps we were going to win. Most of our goal had been accomplished already. The ICHR had received our claim; the AMIA case had become a national and international scandal; the Argentine government feared us. On the other hand, the response embarrassed me, as an Argentinian and as an attorney. I was embarrassed that these people represented my Fatherland. Susana Ruiz Cerrutti, until then a respected member of the Foreign Office and a recognized scholar in the field of international law, signed that paper, perhaps simply because she was in the wrong place at the wrong time; and the incredible clumsiness of the response will haunt her for the rest of her life, likely impeding her hopes of an appointment to the International Court of Justice.

The response was absolutely empty of all legal content, and merely asserted that Argentina had done everything necessary to investigate the case. It went on to claim that the AMIA investigation should be a model for the rest of the world, underlining such remarks with exclamation marks and bold letters. The tone of the response was gravely disrespectful of our party, forgetting that we represented the victims of the bombing. They accused us of seeking publicity and prestige more than the truth. Most remarkable of all, they included a full copy of the whole proceeding, packed in large boxes containing hundreds of volumes of the main case. Of those volumes, 27 were unknown to us, because the tribunal had neglected to provide us the required photocopies. An additional 53 volumes were annexes related to structural damages, autopsies, and reports from the fire department, none of which we had the opportunity to read.

Perhaps they were foolish enough to believe that the sight of a few dozen boxes would convince the ICHR they had been working. Did they hope to undermine our claim with appearances alone? In fact, it was a gross miscalculation on their part. We had insisted already that Galeano and his personnel were filling thousands of pages with empty investigation. Now, they only provided evidence for our claim; the AMIA case was but an empty shell.

There was an added benefit: Galeano had resisted giving us a full copy of the proceeding, instead providing us only one or two volumes each day. But now, we obtained all the files he had provided the ICHR, which, on top of aiding our investigation, proved that Galeano could have provided the full case already, and so was willfully impeding our work.

Once again, I flew to Washington to read the missing volumes of the case and gather materials for our rebuttal. Imagine how our claim will look to the ICHR when they learn we were required to travel to the United States merely to read the case in its entirety. Having done so, we again began exchanging and editing drafts until we produced a final statement. The result was devastating for Argentina's position.

First, we expressed our deep displeasure with the personal attacks and epithets solely intended to disqualify us, forgetting or ignoring the fact that we represented the victims of the gravest terrorist attack in Argentine history. The Argentine response forgot as well that, owing to the principle of unity, the state itself is a united organism, responsible for the actions and omissions of its agents and dependents. The administration acknowledged the negligence of certain organs, but seemed to conceive of them as alien bodies, freeing the administration itself from liability. In doing so, the government admitted a part of our claim: that it had invented facts in an attempt to disguise the truth. For example, the government denied that the participation of Memoria Activa had been essential to the investigation. By way of explanation, it claimed that of the forty-six measures I had requested, the tribunal had produced eighteen in advance. We would later explain the nature of those eighteen refusals, but the government at least seemed to recognize that nearly thirty of those measures were not produced, despite the means and tools at the tribunal's disposal.

Elsewhere they stated that certain measures we requested had been produced already, but a comparison of the dates of our request and their production will prove otherwise. They also falsely claimed to have notified us of certain hearings and, worse, claimed the previous investigation of the Embassy bombing had been proper and the security at the AMIA building was sufficient. Remarkably, their rebuttal of our claim was an argument based on quantity more than quality. They claimed, for instance, that the best proof of its investigative efforts were the hundreds of volumes submitted to the ICHR, or that our own claim had been endorsed "only" by the individual victims rather than the central Jewish institutions. We simply responded that the quantity of their casefiles contributed nothing to the investigation's results.

Yet above all, nothing could be compared with their claim that the investigation "was an exceptional example of world-class investigation [sic]." Such an assertion made me think that Galeano himself had help to draft the response. Who else would claim such a stupidity? Who else would think to defend the indefensible? To rebut the state's response, we went step-by-step through our initial submission, elaborating on their claims and explaining what they had hidden or ignored. For example, with reference to our claim that the failed investigation of the Embassy bombing had enabled the AMIA attack to take place, they asserted that they had in fact begun a meticulous investigation immediately following that first attack. They however failed to mention the fact that after eight years nothing had resulted from that investigation, failing not only to produce a single suspect, but even to explain how the attack on the Embassy had been carried out.

They acknowledged that the AMIA building required security, yet ignored the fact that the police cruiser installed there was disabled, without a functioning battery, and the officers used walkie-talkies provided by AMIA itself. The state ignored, too, that the building's security officers were only declared as witnesses four years after the bombing, and that the relevant logbook had been adulterated. In accordance with the Argentine legal system, any public official who has witnessed a crime or received information pertaining to said crime has the obligation to testify. However, neither the police forces working with the tribunal nor the tribunal itself denounced the falsification of the logbooks; when Memoria Activa pointed out this circumstance, the tribunal responded that we should pursue the crime ourselves.

We underlined the fact that Galeano's many resources did not produce any manner of beneficial result. And the state called this an "unprecedented effort." We had mentioned this in our original claim, and it was undisputed. The issue was the extent to which these failings qualified as reckless disregard. Five years after the attack, our working knowledge was more or less the same as it had been in the immediate aftermath.

According to the Argentine legal system, it is the prosecutor's duty to investigate criminal matters. However, in the AMIA case, not only had the three official prosecutors been engaged in suspicious parallel investigations, but they had failed to control the investigative judge who was willfully hindering the inquiry. We analyzed the state's proposed measures for collecting evidence, and found that every one was either useless or inappropriate. The most notorious of their propositions was that they travel to the United States or Europe, France or Switzerland, to meet a prosecutor or a member of the FBI, or a repentant witness who might bring some clue to the investigation—and every time, having gone with money provided by the taxpayers, they returned with nothing new.

The state also tried to dispute our assertions regarding numerous irregularities in the investigation. For instance, we decried that the samples of dirt used to direct the explosion had been lost forever; Argentina responded that such presumptions were unfounded, and claimed that the results of the Fire Department's report on the matter had been attached to the proceeding on September 29, 1998. However, as we underlined in our rebuttal, the state thus confessed that the report was prepared four years after the explosion, and omitted to clarify that we had been requesting this information since 1997; Galeano was then forced to order the production of that evidence. Worse, when the report arrived, not only were they unable to reach any conclusion, but they suggested the tribunal consult another expert.

In a similar line of thought, we condemned the gross lack of diligence exhibited in the recovery of the van's remains from the rubble. The state believed that in a short time they succeeded in accurately identifying the vehicle. That was not true. The pieces recovered from the AMIA building included a pair of deformed metal rims, dampers, the motor engine, and a collection of twisted metal pieces believed to belong to the chassis of the vehicle. Meager results indeed, and though perhaps sufficient to identify the model of the van, it was not yet enough to identify with certainty the particular vehicle, much less its owner.

We also declared that autopsies of the victims listed incorrect blood types—as was the case with Diana Malamud's husband, for instance—and added that the Jewish religion forbids the exhumation of a buried body. The state ignored this accusation entirely. The sloppiness of the investigation reached its climax with respect to the debris of the AMIA building, piled without order in an empty lot. The state acknowledged that these piles were left without any form of security, and that after three years in the open air, subjected to all forms of weather, were swept into the river. We also underlined in our original claim that several pieces of evidence were lost forever with the tribunal's complicity. That was explained by the state answer as a regrettable mistake obliged by the hurried pace of the investigation. Yet it was impossible to explain the loss of sixty tapes from both the police precinct and SIDE's offices at once.

We had to expand our presentation as the year wore on. In the first months of 2000, we added two new materials in particular, one concerning the systematic loss of evidence on the part of the tribunal, and the other concerning several newly released films documenting Galeano's negotiations with Telleldin.

In the meantime, the general elections took place. In December 1999, after a decade of Peronist rule, the Radical Party's Fernando de la Rua assumed office. Thus, the new administration would judge our response to the former's statements, and they would certainly not want to be implicated in Menem's mess.

After so many battles, so many interviews, so many statements to the press, we at last believed our mantra would prevail: *Justice, justice shall you pursue.*

Finally, I recall a conversation with Muellen, Nisman and Barbaccia, who had aided in Galeano's cover-up. I admitted we might not be able to find the true perpetrators of the attack, but I promised them, looking directly into their eyes, to bring to justice every single collaborator that had impeded their discovery. The time to pay their debts was near. They were shocked.

Toward the end of October 2000, at midday, a young fellow intercepted Pablo and me as we emerged from our offices. He introduced himself as Claudio Lifschitz, a former assistant attorney for Galeano's tribunal from 1995 to 1997. He said we were one hundred percent correct in our suspicions of a cover-up. He offered to provide us all the information he could. Pablo and I looked at each other.

Claudio Lifschitz

It was too good to be true: a former coworker of Galeano's was providing us just the proof we needed. We were cautious, and distrusted such sudden providence. The administration might have changed, but the personnel at SIDE had not, and we assumed Lifschitz was one of them. He was in his early 30's, spoke quickly and jumbled his words. But he looked sincere, and he understood our reluctance. He offered to provide a statement whenever we'd like, but he did not request any compensation in return. "Nothing to lose. Just hear me out," he said. We went to a restaurant across the street. We questioned him about his knowledge and loyalties, and he affirmed that Galeano was following Menem's order to cover up everything. We questioned him as I imagine a policeman interrogates a suspect: taking every angle, questioning every answer, checking and double-checking every word against our information. The guy was a rock. He said he had been intimidated by a group of SIDE agents, but also maintained good contacts with another group. He insisted they had failed to stop him. He was licensed to carry a weapon, and he wasn't afraid of them. He had connections with the intelligence services. He even admitted that his appointment to Galeano's tribunal had been affected through his connection with the current Secretary of Intelligence. He knew everything Galeano had done to conceal the case, and had collected information until his departure from the tribunal. We learned, for instance, that not only had Galeano taped his negotiations with Telleldin, but many other incidents as well. In fact, every person within Galeano's office was recorded on tape: Galeano had hidden a camera behind his hat rack. Muellen, Barbaccia and Nisman used a similar system, and taped every interrogation performed in their offices. All of this had of course been done without the knowledge or express consent of the filmed subjects, a circumstance both unorthodox and without much legal precedent. In a way, such behavior was unlawful; we had already condemned similarly unorthodox methods before the ICHR. We learned that after receiving the footage from Ribelli, Galeano worried over his remaining tapes, and ordered them burned in the garden of one of his assistant's homes. Lifschitz had been engaged mostly with the international connections to the bombing; he was well-informed of Syrian and Iranian activities, which Galeano presumed had had something to do with the attack. That was not our objective. We understood that his knowledge of events within the tribunal was invaluable.

Lifschitz had self-published a book about the case. It is a confused and twisting text, attempting to explain by hints and suggestions more than direct language, the international connections of the AMIA bombing. The book brought us no further information, but it did contain the transcription of Galeano's tape negotiating with Telleldin, as well as some explanations of such things as "page 114" and the investigation of the lot where the van had been parked on July 15. The transcription corresponded to the tape which Cuneo Libarona gave to Ribelli. Had he stolen the tape from the tribunal safe? We didn't care very much. We were looking for information, and Claudio told us that the tape known by the public was only one of several.

Lifschitz later appeared before the Commission of the Congress, offering a complete testimony ratifying our accusation that Galeano was willfully impeding the investigation. We submitted a copy of his testimony to the ICHR, and used this to request Galeano's removal from the case. But that was not going to bring about immediate results.

Our rebuttal of Argentina's statement to the Inter-American Commission devastated Galeano and the new authorities. We rejected their personal attacks and insinuations, the obscure language and excuses to evade liability; and we counterattacked, providing the ICHR with the evidence Lifschitz had provided us, plus whatever information I could glean from the volumes I had yet to read. That was the result of my studies during my long stay in Washington.

Alberto Zuppi with Mirta Lipzyc (left) and Adriana Reisfeld (right)

But that was somehow the end of the road for our case: the evidence we collected was so formidable, it was impossible to deny.

De la Rua could not abide by the former administration's statement if he hoped to evade implication in the cover-up. He and his new administration called for a conciliatory meeting at the Inter-American Commission, where it was agreed that prosecution of our claim would be postponed until the oral trial, and that the President of the Inter-American Commission would be present during the whole trial to elaborate upon a report to the

Commission. This was acceptable. It was clear that all things we had discovered by reading the proceeding would be confirmed during the trial.

In the meantime, the survivors of the bombing, together with the friends and relatives of the deceased, were divided in two groups. On one side was the group consisting of Memoria Activa, Pablo, and myself. We were the rebels, the protesters, the ones going to the press and denouncing the cover-up.

The second group, consisting of those who were not in Memoria Activa, at first maintained a passive role in the case, supporting the private prosecutors for AMIA and DAIA. Later I read an article in an American journal published by a member of the Jewish community, explaining that I was the reason for this division: I was a gentile, and the latter group preferred the representation of Jewish institutions. When the oral trial began to approach, Dobniewsky, AMIA's attorney, submitted to Galeano a series of documents wherein victims or their families requested a part in the proceedings as private prosecutors. This was a strategic move from AMIA, intended to prove they not only represented these institutions, but represented the victims themselves. If they presented enough people, Galeano might decide to unify the private prosecution with AMIA and DAIA, leaving us subject to their will. That was clearly unacceptable, and we began a strange race to present our own requests.

Around that time, we received a call from Itzhak Aviran, the Israeli Ambassador to Argentina, inviting me and Pablo to a meeting at the Israeli Embassy. After the devastation of the Embassy in Arroyo Street, the Israeli Embassy relocated to a skyscraper near *La Casa Rosada*, the executive mansion and office of the President. Security was tight. Members of the Federal Police were at the basement and the Mossad or a private Israeli agency were in charge of the security. We were brought to an upper floor where we would meet Aviran. We waited a couple of minutes before the Ambassador arrived. His face was well known in Argentina, having visited Menem several times and recording for the media those meetings. He was middle-aged, grey-haired and was dressed with a grey suit. Two members of security remained with him during the meeting.

After the formal greetings Aviran went directly to the point: "I wanted to talk with you both because we are approaching the oral trial," Aviran said, "and it will be very important that the private prosecutors join efforts together." Clearly that explained Dobniewsky's strategy of division. Both private prosecutors having more or less the same number of members, Galeano could not unify the prosecution with AMIA and DAIA because, leaving us aside, he would cause a scandal of unpredictable consequences—ours being the only group vocally opposed to his performance.

"No problem," I said. "You can inform the people of AMIA and DAIA that they are welcome to work with us."

Aviran smiled, grimacing. "Well, that was not exactly what I was thinking."

Itzhak Avirán, the Israeli Ambassador to Argentina between 1993-2000

"Well then, let us know when they have decided," I said. The meeting finished quickly, and Pablo and I left. Stepping into the elevator, we looked each other, and began to laugh

10

ON TRIAL

It is a stipulation of Argentine judicial procedure that before a case be moved forward from the written to the oral stage, the investigative judge must issue a formal declaration that sufficient evidence has been collected. Perhaps this evidence would not be sufficient to obtain a proper conviction, but it might detain the indicted in jail, to ensure his presence in the courtroom when his testimony should be required. At this point the opposing parties can propose new evidence to be obtained, or else will consent to the judge's decision. When Galeano informed us of his intention to close the investigation and move to the oral stage, we initially opposed him; it was difficult to consent to the conclusion of a process we did not believe had even truly begun. Nevertheless, after discussing the matter with our clients, we agreed that continuing to request measures that Galeano would never accept was not going to accomplish anything. At the least, exposing Galeano's poor work to the public would enable us to deconstruct the official story he had invented around the AMIA case, to undermine the tribunal's claim to efficiency and to prove that an investigation, in fact, had never properly taken place.

Overcoming our initial reluctance, our next concern was to

determine whether the oral trial would not be a mere continuation of Galeano's comedy. We didn't want to accept such a change only to remain in the same situation. We wanted a proper investigation—or else, we wanted to prove that the investigative work performed so far was a failure.

We were concerned with another aspect of the tribunal. A sense of collegiate solidarity had always existed among judges of the same branch. We didn't know whether such *esprit de corps* would be evident during the oral phase of the trial. We didn't know what to expect at all from the three new federal judges appointed to the case, but we were assuaged after a short inquiry: all three were well regarded by our colleagues, not only as judges, but as jurists as well. One of the judges appointed to *Tribunal Oral Federal Numero 3*, or TOF 3, had to be replaced, but his successor had better academic credentials, having been an assistant professor on the Law Faculty of the University of Buenos Aires, teaching a course on human rights. But the path of federal justice in Argentina is never certain, no matter what in truth is just and fair.

Beyond these concerns over the oral stage, the question remained: what could we expect of the trial? What was our goal, and what was the minimum we could expect to achieve? Arriving at a clear answer to each of these questions was crucial for determining our strategy: we believed the disparity alone between Galeano's work the past seven years and simple legal common sense would be sufficient to prove beyond all doubt his willful obstruction. In that case, the investigation as a whole would be severely damaged; certain documents would be declared null and void, and functionaries would likely be prosecuted. It would be necessary to start the process over, with a clean slate. Despite the passing of time and the irreversible loss of evidence, a fresh start would redirect the investigation toward the real events of the case. We warned our clients of this possibility, and they agreed. It would be best to simply restart, rather than to attempt an escape from the juridical labyrinth. There was always the possibility, too, that during the oral trial some new information would emerge, and a new path might open up, leading to a greater revelation. Clearly either alternative offered a better outcome than our current reality, even considering all possible results between success and failure. Galeano had answered every one of our complaints and requests with a simple *"téngase presente"*—this issue, too, we presented to the ICHR. Being realistic after seven years, we hardly expected to obtain any productive result or to revive the investigation, especially when those in charge were still doing everything in their power to destroy evidence and obscure all investigative lines.

The immediacy of the oral trial provoked the interest of the national and international media. Beyond a queue of metal grids in front of the court building, serving as protective barriers along the pavement, several news vans were parked already, and reporters were scouring the area for interviews. More than four hundred journalists, three hundred of them foreigners, had requested accreditation to be present during the proceedings, obliging the tribunal to postpone the trial until September 2001. The press considered the few clues leaked from the oral tribunal and the parties, and speculated that more than 1400 witnesses were going to be called, placing the length of the trial somewhere between seven and ten months. We knew their predictions were wrong: it would be impossible for any court to complete such a task in less than ten months. We thought it most likely that the trial would take a couple of years, but we didn't mention this in any of the several interviews we gave to the press. We would need the press when the moment arrived to push the public opinion; this was not the time to quell a freshly risen media storm.

The Federal Tribunals of Comodoro Py, named for the street where they were located, occupied the former headquarters of one of the major railway lines in the country. It was located in a sparsely populated quarter of Buenos Aires, near the docks and shipyards, at a distance that many attorneys found an inconvenience for being far away from Plaza Lavalle. Built in the 1940's, it exemplified the architecture of its time: huge halls, large marble corridors, and wide white marble staircases.

The Tribunals in Comodoro Py

In one corner of the basement, a medium-sized theater formerly used for ceremonies had been specially refurbished for the trial. When we first visited the place before the trial began, we felt a mix of strange emotions in that room smelling of fresh paint and wax. On the one hand, we couldn't help but admit a certain solemnity in observing the future setting of the AMIA trial, the most important criminal case in Argentina since the prosecution of the Juntas. On the other hand, the ambiance of that desolate basement room was somehow surreal. New light brown fabrics covered the lower half of the high walls, framing a film screen at the front of the room. There were wooden panels along the stage, brand new seats—some of them still wrapped in plastic—and fixed desks; an Argentine flag was strung to a pole and a crucifix was mounted on the wall, as is usual in public offices. A scaled replica of the Pasteur Street buildings had been installed on a six-foot long table in front of the stage, even the vehicles parked along Pasteur and the light poles on the sidewalk. The model of the AMIA building was removable, in order to show how things looked before and after the explosion.

The judges were to occupy a semicircular stage, with a witness box—in fact only a single chair—to their left, and the court secretary seated to their right. The floor of the theater would be divided between the defense and prosecution, while a thick panel of bulletproof glass separated the rear seats, where relatives of the deceased would sit. An upper level was reserved for the press, the police in charge of recording the trial, and the public. No photo or video cameras were to be allowed. The trial was going to be recorded, and transcriptions of the proceedings were to be distributed among the parties. The defense, seated to the right side of the room, were the most numerous group, with twenty-two defendants and their attorneys. The prosecution on the left occupied a triangular area, with the public prosecutors at the front with us of Memoria Activa, and the private prosecutors for AMIA and DAIA at the rear.

The president of the Inter-American Commission of Human Rights would also sit near the prosecution. Dean Grossman could not possibly attend all the sessions, and so the ICHR had appointed a young attorney named Maria Lousteau to take his place, sitting at the president's side.

Dean Claudio Grosman, President of the Inter American Commission of Human Rights

It was not so impressive as the opening day of Nuremberg had likely been, but it nonetheless represented some work; the new administration clearly intended to adequately supply this trial, which would be so closely scrutinized at home and abroad.

Maria Lousteau will represent Dean Grosman during the trial

The beginnings of the trial would be quickly overshadowed by the brutal attack on the Twin Towers. In Buenos Aires, we watched with dismay the live footage of New York. The senseless attack engendered immediate solidarity with the victims and their families. We couldn't help but observe its similarities to the AMIA incident. It touched us deeply. The images of debris covering the areas we knew so well, where we had been with our own friends and relatives, were profound and saddening. For the victims of the AMIA attack and their families, they were a painful reminder of the tragedy that had struck their own city, seven years earlier.

Finally, the day arrived. The hall was filled. The defendants arrived with their counselors. The state provided public advocates to defend the accused police officers, with the exception of Ribelli, who appointed a private counselor. It was the first time we saw the defendants in person. Polite nods and handshakes passed among colleagues.

The first day of the trial

Among the public were some interesting characters: Telleldin's wife Ana, Galeano (for a short while), and Jorge de la Rua, brother of the president and then-Secretary of Justice; Nisman's wife, also a federal judge, attended, as well as members of AMIA, and more from Memoria Activa. The remaining attendees were seated on the upper floor, together with the press and the officers tasked with recording and transcribing the trial.

At 2:20 PM, all eyes fell on the ancillary Secretary of the Tribunal, who announced that the trial was to begin. Everybody stood upon the entrance of the judges: Pons, Gordo, and Larrandebere. Argentine judges do not wear robes, hats or wigs. Our one tradition might be that all parties, including the members of the Tribunal, dress formally, wearing jackets and ties or, like the members of the TOF 3 in their first session, dark suits. I always liked the distinctive symbolism of the robe, such as judges in the U.S. or Germany wear. It would seem to suggest that we were not attending to an everyday situation; this was a solemn act of justice, and not a simple legal errand.

The presiding judge ordered the commencement of the session—but before the prosecution could speak, Pablo stood and respectfully asked permission to make a request. With the judge's consent, Pablo said:

The Oral Chamber: Judges Larrandebere, Pons and Gordo

"*Your Honor, Memoria Activa would ask the court before the trial's start to observe a respectful minute of silence in memory of the AMIA victims, the victims of the Israeli Embassy, and the victims of the recent attack against the Twin Towers.*"

The first day of the oral trial: A minute of silence

Such a request was unprecedented, but who would refuse such a tribute to the victims of terrorism, especially before the media? The members of the Tribunal looked surprised, but they shortly agreed. It was a clever public act that would be reported by the press. A more formal and strict tribunal could have refused such kind of homage as inappropriate within an impartial court of justice, but the surprise of the request and the pressure of the 400 journalists were sufficient to accept it. Telleldin's counselor, commenting to the press later that day, summarized that moment like the results of a soccer match: *Memoria Activa: 1, Us: 0.*

Alberto Nisman, the appointed prosecutor for the oral trial, opened with a reading of his statement. Muellen and Barbaccia were seated beside him. A handsome young man, Nisman, together with an older colleague, then represented the Public

Ministry, an organ synonymous with Public Prosecution. I was convinced, along with members of Memoria Activa, that Nisman was a part of Galeano's gang. He had already been involved with certain of the suspicious activities perpetrated by Galeano and his prosecutors, such as filming without legal authorization or the consent of the subject. He was defending and representing the official story. Pablo, who had greater exposure to federal justice than I, was more condescending toward Nisman.

Official prosecution: Romero, Nisman, Barbaccia and Muellen

Nisman, too, was Jewish, and Pablo believed he should have behaved differently in the investigation of such an anti-Semitic attack. I was not convinced of the merits of such an argument, having witnessed the behavior of other members of the Jewish community, but it was not a point for discussion now.

When, after so much anticipation, the reading finally began, a feeling of anticlimax spread through the hall. The press and public had clearly expected to witness cross interrogations, to hear the defendants speak and to learn of the case's dramatic evolution. The monotonous reading of the

Part of the accused with their counsellors

accusation, which would occupy the entire first week, frustrated them. The reading was necessary, however; the indictments were the core of the proceeding. After the initial statements, there followed a reading of the accusations by the private prosecutors, and then a summary of Galeano's closure of the investigation, including all scripts in relation with that fact.

In the third week, the defendants began to make their statements. In the terms set out within the Argentine legal code—just as those of the United States'—any person accused of a crime may choose to remain silent, and this silence will not permit the presumption of his or his guilt. However, if, during the declaration, the defendant for whatever reason decides to lie, even if the lie is discovered, the defendant cannot be indicted for perjury. In other words—and although we borrowed much of the American Constitution as the inspiration for our own—under Argentine law, a defendant's lie has no consequences; the crime of perjury does not exist.

This is a grave misinterpretation of the individual's right to evade self-incrimination. During my time in the Senate, as counselor to certain legislators, I had prepared several projects to include perjury in our criminal law—but the senators I had counseled lacked the political weight to impose such a project. Telleldin's case gave me the perfect opportunity to demonstrate the errors of the Argentine system. He had already testified six times before Galeano, and each time offered a different story. Telleldin lied openly, brazenly, without any further consideration: he did not simply lie, but suggested a planned and premeditated attempt to derail the investigation, which in my opinion surpasses any possible right to avoid self-incrimination.

When the tribunal called Telleldin to the witness box, a murmur spread through the hall. After all, he was the only genuine local connection to the bombing, and his statement was of utmost importance. Dressed in a suit, short of height and with a head too large for his body—which explained his nickname of *Enano*, or Dwarf—he walked slowly to the box. When the President of the Tribunal asked whether he had any nicknames, Telleldin hesitated after saying, "No". "Some people call me Charly, or *Enano*," he continued. After being asked to share what he knew of the case, Telleldin responded with a statement he perhaps should have used before, in place of his lies: "By counsel of my attorney I prefer not to declare." His attorney, seated on the parterre, moved his lips, saying, "For now", but Telleldin had already left the witness box, excused by the President. Judge Pons, who was presiding, ordered the Secretary to read aloud all previous declarations from Telleldin, to be added to the current acts. That was the only declaration we had anticipated. Telleldin had testified six times before Galeano, and each time offered a different version of events. He was an experienced criminal, with a long list of prior run-ins with the law; he was used to playing the best position he could obtain, especially when nobody else knew the truth but him. We expected the new scenario to perhaps bring a different perspective out of him, but we were wrong. Hearing his former declarations, you might understand his technique of undaunted lying, mixing a couple of real events with lies, moving the investigation one step forward and ten steps back.

The rest of the day and the following week concerned the testimonies of the remaining defendants, all of them police officers we had never accused, whose indictment was in our opinion an invention of Galeano's. Only Telleldin's second testimony, wherein he accused the officers of extortion, had been used to incriminate them. No other link connected them to the van used for the explosion. Telleldin being a consummate liar, it was impossible to credit any degree of verisimilitude to his story.

When the readings and the presentation of the accused finished, the Tribunal ordered the projection of the videotape of Galeano dealing with Telleldin. The first video was projected on the screen. This was the footage Ribelli had obtained from somebody inside the tribunal, later released to the public by the journalist Jorge Lanata, then Pablo's own client.

The darkened hall watched the footage in silence. Galeano offered to intermediate between "some people" who were interested in supporting the payment of US $400,000 to Telleldin. In order to camouflage the bribe, Telleldin said he was writing a book and the money could be its payment. Galeano then passed a paper across the table to Telleldin: "*Listen to me... hum... this person who is interested in buying the book... the only thing that he wants to know is whether you can answer this. You can answer yes or no.*" Telleldin read the paper and began speaking quickly, in confused and jumbled sentences: "*I will tell you what I will do. I want the money deposited at the Lloyd in Cabildo. I will transfer three hundred and fifty thousand to Colonia, Uruguay, facing the Argentine Embassy to the bank that it is there. I will let the money sit in a fixed deposit to obtain fifty thousand dollars.*" Galeano nervously replied that he didn't want to speak of that subject. Telleldin interrupted him: "*...there is a contract, it is sold, the book is delivered. We will have an interview to finish the part you are interested in. I will testify at the trial. Besides, the case lacks some fundamental witnesses, the most important ones.*" "*OK. See if something is lacking,*" said the judge. Telleldin promised to testify once the payment was complete.

The video ran for a good hour and a half, and all along Telleldin mixed up truth and fiction, making an incoherent narrative of it all. It was clear he was improvising, undermining all clarity, scattering information in order to confuse his listener. The judge smoked one cigarette after another and toyed with the pack, seeming to follow Telleldin's verbal somersaults with all his attention. He was clearly growing impatient, and wanted to return the conversation to the track he had set. But Telleldin was playing a game he had perfected in the course of his life: he acted friendly and helpless, more than willing to comply, but in fact he was in charge of the conversation. He delayed any possible conclusions, saying he might be able to answer certain questions, but others he could not; and even regarding those he might answer, he would need to provide evidence—a practical impossibility, but one he would attempt nonetheless. Despite being imprisoned for more than three years by the time the video had been recorded, he seemed to be in no hurry; it was nothing new for him. He was accustomed to prison, the special treatment:

exchanging favors, visits from his wife and children, with time left to study law. He spoke in circles, never finally answering what was asked of him. His witnesses were fearsome, he said, and they were not prepared to speak with anybody. "*Least of all with you,*" he said, looking at Galeano. "*You are worse than the devil to them.*" Galeano perhaps realized then that he had fallen into Telleldin's web, but he persisted in his attempts to obtain something that would reassure his "people." He opened the door to another series of offers, acknowledging that would be perhaps possible to fulfill, but perhaps would be extremely difficult, and so on. Garbage. Nothing was there, absolutely nothing. It was one hour and a half of babbling, repetitions and confusion. At the end of the film, it was clear nothing of value could be extracted from the video other than to watch the exchanges of a weak judge and a cheeky defendant.

Following the end of the film, and the requisite pause to gather ourselves, a second video was projected. This footage was certainly worse for Galeano than the first: now, he and his deputies presented Telleldin an album containing photos of the police officers Telleldin was to identify as his blackmailers. He had violated all principles of due process, and it was captured on film. It was bad enough the judge had negotiated a payment to his detainee in exchange for information; even worse, that he had orchestrated the detainee's own testimony.

During the projection, I observed Maria Lousteau taking notes. *Good*, I thought, *we are doing well*. Even the officers and their counselors were smiling: these videos proved the collusion of Galeano and Telleldin, the only two men opposed to their freedom.

The projection of those two videos might have been a turning point in the tribunal, though we didn't realize it at the time. The footage proved beyond any doubt that something unorthodox had occurred during the investigation. We had discussed those videos previously, but the circumstance of their projection in the courtroom, before the press and the public and the three new judges, had a profound effect on all that was to follow. Everything that would be shown during the trial would be tainted by the illegal behavior of the men who led the investigation. If for whatever reason Galeano had up to now maintained his position, his activities would now be seriously questioned. Profiting from the increased scrutiny, we requested of the Chamber of Appeals in a separate proceeding, that Galeano and his public prosecutors be immediately barred from the AMIA investigation and all other proceedings. This request, too, appeared the next day in the news reports.

That first day of witness testimonies began the surprises for the case. One of the initial problems with the investigation had been the lack of witnesses of the white Trafic van prior to the blast. It was strange that something could have occurred during a busy morning in a crowded quarter of the city, without anyone having seen it. Nobody had even heard the inevitable noise of the van ascending the sidewalk and crushing the doors of the AMIA. Nobody. Not even a casual driver behind the van, nor a passenger of one of the many buses passing along Pasteur, nor a pedestrian had seen anything. We believed those witnesses, assuming they existed, had never been sufficiently sought or had perished in the blast.

Only one pedestrian witness gave some general information about a slow-moving van that nearly hit her when she was crossing Tucuman Street at the corner of the AMIA building. She said she was bringing her son to school with her sister, when the boy suddenly ran ahead to the street corner to pass the vehicle. The child probably saved their lives: his sudden movement obliged her to run after him, mere seconds in advance of the explosion. They had taken no more than six steps after crossing the street when the blast hit them from behind. In her first testimony, some weeks after the event, she had given a vague description of the van's driver, who for a moment looked at her when turning the corner. The description was used to produce an identikit. However, seven years later, she gave a new testimony, describing the driver more accurately, with short black hair and dark eyes, stating that the identikit was not very similar to the person she had seen. Moreover, she stated that the van she had seen had no lateral door. That point was important, because one of the few parts collected among the rubble was a twisted piece of the van's lateral door. The door also made the difference between the original body of the van bought by Telleldin, which contained the motor discovered among the rubble, and the duplicate's body, belonging to a van that never had been found—which would presumably have included a side door. However, the witness was revealing this information only after seven years, and common sense would suggest that such specific detail was unlikely from a person who had only confirmed the van was a Trafic because her child said so. "*I understand nothing of cars*", she explained to the judges. Her sister and her child hadn't seen anything. Even a young man who came to their aid after the blast, when they fell onto the sidewalk, hadn't seen a thing. In addition, this woman had always described the van as beige rather than white. This was another reason to take her testimony with special precaution.

Another witness who mentioned the van was a man who worked as an attendant near the AMIA building. He claimed to have seen the van at the same corner as the prior witness. However, he had seen the van from the opposite corner of the block, one hundred and fifty yards away, while he was crossing the street. When the judges interrogated him, he contradicted some details of his initial statement. This was especially noted by one of the attorneys for the police officers, who did not believe the van existed, thinking instead that the bomb had been planted within the AMIA building or within the container placed at the AMIA's front. The cross interrogation of both witnesses didn't cast much light onto the issue. However, the latter witness mentioned a circumstance that brought horror to the hall. He said he had found on a terrace of his building, on the tenth floor, the top part of a human head. A fireman collected the remains later, but no mention of it had been made in the written case. That was how Galeano had led the investigation: nothing new for us, but surprising for several others. Many years later in 2016, the bucket containing those remains mixed with others, would be found frozen in one refrigeration chamber of the morgue. They had not been analyzed until this rediscovery.

After that session, the public prosecution and the representative of AMIA and DAIA were triumphant, insisting these testimonies had proved the existence of the Trafic van. We were not so certain, considering the many gaps and contradictions in their statements, not to speak of the seven years that had elapsed since the events described. In fact, we were the only ones who had achieved anything substantial that day, because we were able to show how poor the investigation had been so far. How was it those witnesses had not been intensively questioned before? How was it possible the identikit of the van's driver performed shortly after the attack was so far afield of what the witness now recalled? How could we explain the fact that human remains recovered from a neighboring building hadn't been mentioned in any report? Were there more victims than had been originally estimated? All these questions reflected the clumsiness of the investigation, and we saw that the representative of the ICHR had been taking down detailed notes of all these incidences.

The next day, another group of witnesses who were close to the blast site testified, but none of them could confirm the existence of the Trafic van. That was one point for the defense, because if the existence of the van could not be proven beyond all doubt, that would suggest that neither Telleldin nor the police officers had anything to do with the attack.

The most dramatic testimony heard during those days was, beyond any doubt, that of Rosa Montano. She was bringing her five-year-old son to his kindergarten that day. They had just passed the door of the AMIA building when, she said, "a kind of strong wind lifted me up and threw me away. I couldn't breathe. I wanted to see where my son was. I wanted to wake him up." Then she said she saw her son lying down on the floor one meter behind her, but she couldn't lift up him. "My right arm had an open fracture, muscles and sinews were torn. My hand was hanging off." She saw how the people lifted her son. "I wanted to follow him, but I couldn't," she said between sobs and tears. She was hospitalized more than a month. "I couldn't bury my son," she explained. Rosa Montero had not seen a van, nor did she hear any vehicle climb the sidewalk. She was accurate in describing the other vehicles on Pasteur, and recalled events in great detail. She described the container in front of the AMIA building being filled up with debris from the renovations, and she recalled a man pushing his stalled vehicle. How could Rosa be so accurate, yet be unable to remember something so notable? We were convinced of the existence of the Trafic van, and we couldn't help but wonder at the number of people—and all of them with detailed memories of that day—who had disregarded the vehicle entirely.

A relevant testimony for the defense was produced by a survivor of the explosion, who had nearly lost his right eye. He insisted he hadn't seen any Trafic van, despite being near the entrance of the AMIA building when the bomb went off, pushing his stalled car. He said he had opened the hood of his car, glanced for a brief moment at the AMIA entrance, and then returned to the motor of his vehicle at the precise moment of the explosion. "A blaze struck me head-on."

But the existence of the Trafic van would be proved dramatically with the photographs and testimony of one of the forensics experts who examined the corpses following the explosion. He stated that one of the van's dampers had been found imbedded in the vertebral spine of a victim, which could never have been done without the strength of an explosion to propel the object. This testimony discarded all theories such as those supported by members of the defense, claiming that the parts of the van had been planted among the rubble.

There were also six different expert reports: from the Argentine Federal Police, from the National Gendarmerie, from a specialized American agency, a German agency, an Israeli agency and a private agency commissioned by two journalists. All of them agreed that the cause of the explosion was a bomb placed within a Trafic van. The tribunal seemed to have been also involved in the doubt and questions surrounding the van. They ordered a chemical analysis of the motor, to determine whether it had been affected by such extreme temperatures as would be caused in an explosion. When the report arrived in November 2001, the expert's conclusion was positive. In December, two previously unheard-of witnesses, residents near the AMIA building, claimed to have heard a heavy vehicle stopping just before the explosion. Another woman heard somebody shout, "*Stop it, it's going to kill us!*" but even such testimonies, performed seven years after the event, cannot be considered solid evidence.

In November 2001, the case seemed to have reached a plateau, and even press attendance to the sessions grew sporadic. Dozens of witnesses testified as to their whereabouts at the moment of the explosion. They touched the audience deeply, as though we were hearing from our own families. We learned the destiny of people walking along Pasteur Street that day, mutilated by falling glass and debris, or otherwise impaired for the remainder of their lives, physically or mentally. We learned of the volunteers in the immediate aftermath, how they remained hours removing debris, and of their triumph when they finally uncovered a survivor beneath the rubble. However, in spite of those accounts of suffering and courage, the people attending the trial grew bored.

The tribunal was going to take years. It was difficult for the press to sustain public interest in a case with no visible progress. Our own perspective was different, because we already understood the poverty of the investigation. We expected little of the trial. If something new arrived from the interrogations, it would be welcome. At least public opinion—as well as the opinion of the ICHR—confirmed what we had known already: the AMIA case was a farce.

We received weekly transcriptions of the interrogations. The Federal Police performed their work rather ineptly: the names of the witnesses, of the interrogators, and even our own names were misspelled. I never understood why we were not using a stenographer. They were used in Legislative sessions at the Congress. Another gap in Argentine criminal proceeding.

The second week of November began with the testimonies of the police officers charged with patrolling the AMIA building. It was clear the police cruiser parked in front of the building had lacked a functioning battery for a long while. Not only was the vehicle immobile, but the radio too was useless. Communication with the station was performed on walkie-talkies provided by AMIA itself. The precinct was well aware of the condition of the vehicle. Several Jewish institutions had begun to set up short, reinforced concrete poles to prevent a suicide bomber from crashing into the building. Such protection had not been considered for AMIA. Such inattention is remarkable, especially considering the Embassy bombing two years before.

In the AMIA case, we discovered that the police officer assigned to drive the day before at the blast didn't possess a valid driver's license; worse, he didn't know how to drive. He included some commentaries concerning the night before the blast that made the press of the following day to talk of "mysteries of the AMIA": he described shadows moving along the building which, when he stepped from the useless patrol car and approached, had vanished. He also stated that his shift ended at 6 AM, and the next officer did not arrive until 9 AM—though a 6 AM arrival was falsely noted in the logbook. This confirmed something we had suggested to the ICHR: the logbook was falsified with several scribbles, erasures and a clear application of liquid whiteout.

Due to the cold the morning of the attack, the officers in the stalled cruiser requested a spare battery in order to use the car heater. The senselessness of the useless police cruiser bore some relevance to our argument, because we insisted to the ICHR that the AMIA building's lack of effective security had been one of the reasons the attackers had chosen it for a target. After hearing these testimonies, it was clear to the tribunal and to the ICHR that the car served as no better defense to the building than the container parked at the front of AMIA. Both had to be removed with a crane after the explosion.

Apart from the fact that the officers had been called to testify only twice in seven years, and that several minor details relevant to the investigation had been lost forever, what had been established a hundred times we heard again and again "*I don't remember. I don't recall,*" nothing important. Later, members of the security forces present at the time of the explosion began to testify, as well as those who had arrived in the aftermath to rescue survivors and gather evidence. Because several reports had arrived at the tribunal, a postponement was ordered until December 10, so that they might have time to read.

In December, the Chamber of Appeals accepted our request to exclude Galeano, Muellen, and Barbaccia from further involvement in the AMIA investigation.

11

REVOLUTION

De la Rua's administration upheld much of Menem's policy toward the military. However, public opinion had changed over the years, especially as more and more crimes were uncovered, calling for certain pardoned members of the juntas to be prosecuted once again—now, for new crimes, and questioning as well the legitimacy in international law of those amnesties and pardons given by Menem.

Early in March 2001, I received a call from Pablo Parenti, one of two clerks for Judge Gabriel Cavallo. Cavallo was a friend of Pablo Jacoby's, and invited me to a private meeting in his home, along with Cavallo and other members of his staff.

That evening, there was Cavallo with Hernan Folgueiro, the other clerk of the tribunal, as well as Parenti himself. They said they were working on a case that would derogate Alfonsin's impunity laws, "Final Stop" and "Due Obedience", and they wanted to know my opinion with regard to international criminal law. I was delighted with the idea that those laws might finally be derogated, and I read the full project of decision they prepared for the case of Simon and Del Cerro, two military members who had kidnapped, tortured, and finally murdered Gertrudis Hlackzik and José Poblete. They were especially cruel with José, who had lost his legs: they called him "shorty," and tossed him down the stairs. Cavallo and his clerks had been collecting evidence and prepared a formidable case. We commented together some aspects of the decision related to public international law. That decision, we knew, would be historic.

When the sentence was finally issued, as anticipated, it shocked the nation. Cavallo declared the impunity laws unconstitutional, which would mean that all procedures stopped by those laws would have to be reopened. The press put the issue on the front page of all Argentine newspapers, and, though we expected the sentence would be appealed and probably decided at last by the Supreme Court, it was a breath of fresh air that suggested some potential for change.

Our usual work, meanwhile, continued. Pablo and I not only attended the AMIA sessions, but engaged in many joint and separate cases. The AMIA case certainly took up most of our time, but our work in the courtroom was reduced to occasional cross interrogations, and these only on scheduled days. When we anticipated the testimony of a central witness or suspect, we prepared our questions and possible rebuttals in advance. But such situations were exceptions, the more frequent rule being to either ratify prior testimonies or to hear new ones nonessential to our case. In addition, because criminal proceedings during the instruction period are written, the attorney is able to handle several cases at once.

One case in particular, in which I alone represented the German government, had a special meaning for Argentina, and it was going to have unexpected consequences for me. A German girl visiting Argentina during the dictatorship had had the bad luck of ringing the doorbell of a house under the surveillance of an Operational Group, suspected of harboring terrorists. She was abducted, tortured, raped, and brutally killed. Her father in Germany had to pay the Argentine military for the return of her corpse.

In the midst of the oral trials, I requested the extradition to Germany of three Argentine military members involved in this crime: General Suarez Mason, Main Commander of the Military Army to which the Operational Group belonged, his main subordinate Sasiain, and Duran Saenz, a lesser member of the Group. At the time of my request, they were protected under Alfonsin's legislation.

German Chancellor Gerhard Schröder came to Argentina at the end of August 2001. I had the privilege to meet with him privately, at the Sheraton Hotel where he was staying in downtown Buenos Aires. We had our meeting alone, and he gave me very precise directives concerning the extradition case. He authorized me to go to the furthest consequences in our request, even to appeal in case it was refused. He was absolutely determined to prosecute those men before a German court of law, and I was happy to go as far as I could to bring justice to Argentina. The step was unprecedented. Never before had a country requesting an individual's extradition appealed when the country of residence refused. Usually such events are handled diplomatically, but Chancellor Schröder was determined to put Argentina in a very uncomfortable situation, defending the indefensible.

In my presentation for the extradition before the Argentine Federal judge, I explained that the crimes committed by these individuals were crimes against humanity. According to a mandatory principle of international law concerning crimes against humanity, Argentina was obliged either to concede the extradition of these men to Germany, or to prosecute the requested criminals at home.

In the second week of December 2001, benefitting from the public attention of the AMIA case, I explained the issue in several press interviews.

In those days, my wife received a threatening phone call. An anonymous caller said to my wife: "*Take good care of your children.*" That was especially menacing, because our daughter had been born at the end of November. We presented a denunciation before a federal judge, and obtained a uniformed police officer on the sidewalk outside our building, and tapped our phones. The calls stopped, but the spirit at home was somber.

We were reaching the end of the year. The political situation in Argentina had been deteriorating on a daily basis. To be in the hall, hearing those endless testimonies, made us lose some of our sense of reality. We lived then within a bubble, concentrated on one of the most important criminal cases in Argentina's history—but the outside world continued to progress without our attention.

Despite a decade of corruption at every level of Argentine society, the 1990's saw a miraculous period of some economic stability, with a fixed rate of one Argentine peso to one American dollar; money flowed through the economy thanks to the Peronists' privatization of all public enterprises, which, some suspected, resulted from bribery and the biased favoritism of Menem. Suddenly, modern and imported cars were seen frequently in Buenos Aires; *Dame dos*—"Give me two"—was a phrase oft-heard in Miami, where Argentine tourists were overflowing.

As Alfonsin had struggled, so too did De la Rua. It seemed the Radicals did not possess the political skill of the Peronists to traverse turbulent waters. The country was in turmoil; the government's economic measures were the cause of countless daily protests. In those days, we spoke of the *corralito*, the chicken hen: the government's restriction on the amount of money one could withdraw from his or her bank account on any given day, a clearly unconstitutional prohibition. Banks were surrounded every day by angry crowds, beating the iron shutters and doors, demanding their money. At night, in different corners of the city, spontaneous protestors gathered, banging saucepans and skillets, producing a racket that could be heard across Buenos Aires. The same occurred in all major cities of the country. There was a clear discontent with the De la Rua administration, which had shown itself absolutely unfit to resolve the economic crisis affecting the nation. Our memory was still fresh with the events of a decade before—similar to those arising across the globe—which had then cost Alfonsin his presidency.

The popular protest against De la Rua's economic measures built to a climax, and on December 19, 2001, after protesters looted a supermarket, the president decided to impose martial law. Such lootings had been a central cause of Alfonsin's fall, certainly fueled by the Peronists. De la Rua didn't want to repeat his predecessor's mistakes, but the state of siege produced the opposite reaction that he intended. That night, there was a huge and fairly spontaneous protest across all major cities in the country. In Buenos Aires, several thousand protesters assembled at the Plaza de Mayo, a traditional meeting place due to its proximity to the Casa Rosada and the Cabildo, a colonial building from the times of our independence. The protesters in the Plaza de Mayo banged pans, skillets, and pot lids, making their discontent known by this clamor. There was a common shout in the crowd: "*Everyone must leave!*" meaning that all members of the government, all representatives of the old politics must go. I recall, bringing my mother-in-law home that night, hearing the pans and skillets resounding all throughout our drive.

Crisis of December 2001

By the following morning, the protest had spread—even

though the Minister of Economy, whose confiscatory measures had inspired their discontent, had already resigned. The protesters remained at the Plaza de Mayo for several hours, condemning the government for the country's economic chaos and calling for the resignation of President De la Rua.

Crisis of December 2001

Then, on December 21, without any prior warning, the police forces arrived and brutally attacked those still congregated at Plaza de Mayo. Even the world-renowned "*Mothers of the Plaza de Mayo*," easily identified

by their white headscarves, symbols of peaceful revolt against the dictatorship, were violently corralled by the cavalry. These events were broadcast live on television. Thirty-six people were killed that day. Argentina was in shock. You could feel the tension in the air, a revolutionary spirit alike that which inflated the breasts of the French citizens amidst their barricades; or like the spirit of May 1810 in Argentina, when in the same Plaza de Mayo our own independence began, in a revolt against the Spanish Viceroy.

An authentic, truly popular revolutionary movement was burgeoning, and the occurrence of these events in a place so suggestive of our struggle for independence, as well as the sight of those three dozen

victims, aggravated the already restless spirits of the crowd. De la Rua, who earlier that same day had declared his refusal to resign, hurriedly wrote his letter of resignation, and fled the Casa Rosada by helicopter.

The next day, Congress appointed a temporary government, which would call a general election within sixty days. The newly-appointed interim president was Adolfo Rodriguez Saá, governor of the province of San Luis. Since 1999, I had been working at the Senate as a counselor to Adolfo's brother, Alberto Rodriguez Saá, then senator for San Luis. I had been helping to prepare several projects, concerned particularly with the fulfillment of the national duties on human rights, which had even received the compliments of a member of the ICHR. Alberto had been an effective senator despite being in the opposition party, and his concern over human rights was surprising. Despite the reputation of the Rodriguez Saá family as "caudillos" in their native province, which they had directed for more than two decades, the accomplishment of their government was overwhelming: they changed one of the poorest provinces in Argentina into a modern, orderly and well-oiled machine, working with unsurpassed precision.

After the appointment of his brother to the presidency, Alberto called me at home, asking me to join the transitory government as Secretary of Justice. I was surprised, mainly owing to my self-proclaimed ignorance of politics and my not being a Peronist; in fact, I had voted for De la Rua in the previous election. But the situation in Argentina was so dire, there was not much time to waste on indecision. I accepted the offer. All Ministers assumed office on December 23, 2001.

With little warning, I was shaken from the bubble of the AMIA sessions and placed in the midst of the nation's turmoil. Later, whenever I was asked to comment on that time, I always gave the same response: I felt I had no choice at all. For the first time in my life, my country required my work and attention; I hardly had the time to doubt.

News of my appointment spread quickly to the press; my appearance at the oral session that day was a good opportunity to bring some news to a case that hadn't much interested the public for several weeks. They were the same members of the press who had helped me to relay information to the public. I enjoyed a privileged podium before when I needed it. Now, it was their turn to receive information. Just two weeks earlier, I had been using every conceivable mean to inform the press about the requested extradition of the German girl's three murderers. The question was automatic in my first interview: *"Now, you are the new Secretary of Justice; what are you going to do?"* The point was clear, and not a question of policy. I reaffirmed my position that Alfonsin's legislation violated international law, and that Argentina had only two options: either prosecute, or extradite. In less than a day, and without so desiring, my comments as Secretary of Justice had caused an unexpected problem for the new government. Not only had Rodríguez Saá announced the fallout of the whole Argentine foreign debt, but his Secretary of Justice was promoting an unexpected conflict with the military.

The next day, Christmas Eve, I was summoned to a meeting in the Casa Rosada with Rodriquez Saá, the Minister of Defense, and the three military Chiefs of Staff of the Army, Navy, and Aviation, respectively. They expected an explanation. The meeting was tense; they looked at me as though I were a former member of the guerrillas or some other brand of leftist revolutionary. I explained that I had counseled Rodriguez Saá for several years, and that my answers to the press had been in response to a purely legal question, answerable only with purely legal argument; my statements had nothing to do with my political sympathies. It was a question of the law, indisputable and unavoidable; it was never a statement against the administration. Nobody could expect that Argentina would swim against the currents of international law.

It was a fact that would inevitably be produced, with me or without me, with this President or the next. We were not isolated on this planet, and international law should be followed; and, concerning such crimes against international law as had led to my extradition cases, there are only two options: either we prosecute ourselves the criminals or we extradite them to the country requiring their extradition.

Despite my best efforts, I do not think I finally convinced any one of them. I proposed a new meeting, together with the legal counselors of all three branches of the military, to discuss the issue. I assumed everybody in the room would agree that the revolutionary state in which we then lived was the number one priority, and required the joint efforts of all of Argentine society. We agreed that the Minister of Defense would organize the meeting after Christmas. It was a strange situation indeed. The Peronists used to say that if you want to stop something, just propose a Commission. This meeting would postpone any announcement until the issue had been clarified. I was relenting, without any longer desiring what I had proclaimed the previous week. Strange indeed, but I was convinced the meeting would have a positive outcome; we had deviated, but we would return to the proper, legal path.

The announcement of default made us the economic pariahs of the world. Personally, I was against it, but having now seen the state of things from the inside, I realized we had no other choice. We could not pay the incredible amount of interest inherited from the former administrations.

Rodriguez Saá was convinced that within 60 days we could change the former government's image of expenditure into one of austerity. The state would not provide our cars or cellphones. The only distinctive thing was the bronze license plate number 6, which I carried in my car as Secretary of Justice, and a driver.

Though I did not want somebody else driving my car, it was impossible to arrive at as many places as I needed without somebody else to care for the vehicle.

I retained a security guard at the building where our apartment was located, but I refused such custodianship as ministers tend to have. However, after the first days, the measures imposed were extraordinarily popular according to the surveys we received daily at our office, showing approval ratings of 80% for the transitional government. But the surveys were not only read by members of the government; these numbers worried Duhalde, who wanted, as head of the Peronist Party, to run for President in the coming elections. He realized he had been mistake to authorize the appointment of Rodriguez Saá, who might be able to obtain all the required support to turn his sixty days into four years. I was happy with the evolution, but totally unprepared to remain in office one day more than the sixty assigned. I wanted badly to return to my former life, my family and the AMIA case that burdened Pablo alone.

A separate book could be written on the events of those days; several books were in fact later published on Rodriguez Saá's presidency. All day I was immersed in a maelstrom of activities, beginning at 6 A.M. in my office and continuing without pause until midnight. Even the police custody at the building where the Secretary of Justice was installed had to modify their schedules: when I first arrived, nobody was there even to open the parking lot.

A surprising and certainly unexpected situation came from the people of Memoria Activa. Laura Ginsberg declared to the press their disgust with my appointment as Secretary of Justice. She proclaimed: *Memoria Activa denounces before the ICHR the Argentine state. Now our attorney is a part of the government, of the Argentine state, the denounced state, and this is unacceptable.* When I read the news, I called them to a meeting in my ministerial office.

I couldn't believe the situation was real. As a public official, I had to take some care over what I was going to say.

When we were finally reunited, I assured that I was going to do everything possible from my office to clarify the case. I expressed my disgust over their doubts. How could they imagine that I would behave differently because of my new office? We were claiming against a concealment performed only by one administration, not by the Argentine State, and now, if I have the chance to bring this concealment to light, I was prepared to do so. This was a different administration. The Argentine State would always be responsible for the acts of its officials from current or former administrations, but this had nothing to do with incompatibility. A new administration may bring to light the concealment of a former administration, and if that happens, the claim before the ICHR would be proved. The people of Memoria Activa understood my message. Only Laura remained on the outside, still insisting on my incompatibility. I even recall that once Laura was invited to be part of a list of candidates for the Argentine congress I strongly recommended she accept it. It would be a great help to have somebody inside, within the government, who would be in a better position to officially push for documents or information.

I didn't understand then and I don't understand now what kind of problem Laura imagined at that time, and, so far as I know, she still remains unconvinced. Laura being against the position of the rest of Memoria Activa, she went alone and later founded another organization. It was sad to lose such a person from Memoria Activa, but it seemed that we were speaking different languages.

Pablo was travelling from my offices to the trial several times a day; he knew of my intentions. I had already contacted Carlos Sergnese, a former judge of the Supreme Court of San Luis who was now in charge of SIDE, and requested his help. *"We need to clarify AMIA. We need to know what happened. Check if you can find some of the documents that must have been there and disappeared."* Events, however, imposed their own rhythm. From my new office of the Ministry of Justice in downtown Buenos Aires we had to travel to Olivos, where the presidential residence is located thirty kilometers outside of the city. There, we met with members of the Ministry of Economy; Rodriguez Saá, in accordance with the terms of his appointment, had announced the default of the Argentine foreign debt; we in the Secretary of Justice had to work on the legal aspects of the problems Argentina would soon be confronting. From the Presidential Residence in Olivos, we had to hurry to the tribunals, in order to support the judges investigating the murders that occurred during the lootings and the repression in Plaza de Mayo. Then, back to the office to meet the Ambassador of Sweden, regarding the possibility of reopening the case against a member of the Navy, formerly convicted for the murder of a Swedish girl, who had been pardoned by Menem. The German Ambassador also wanted updates on the extradition of Suarez Mason.

The former Secretary of the ICHR, Jorge Taiana, had resigned from his position in Washington and was living again in Argentina. I couldn't imagine a better deputy for the Secretary of Human Rights, and I asked him to join my team. He accepted, which would be especially useful to me, he being a Peronist, in understanding the Peronists that now filled the Cabinet. A formal ceremony had been prepared at the theatre on the 14th floor of the Ministry, where Taiana took his oath. Then we hurried again to a meeting with members of the Supreme Court, who promised a "governable transition" if we did not mess with them. Madness. It was a hectic time, without pause.

Then, on Saint Sylvester's night, I learned via the press that Rodriguez Saá had resigned. Unbelievable. After only a week, without any prior consultation, he had resigned by television. Easy as that. He said he lacked the political support of the Congress that had elected him. Everything had begun in

Rodriguez Saá's presidential residence in Chapaldmalal, on the coast of the Buenos Aires province, where he had planned to spend Sylvester Night. It seems the lights were suddenly turned off, and the security staff disappeared. Rodriguez Saá feared for his life. He, his brother, and the members of the Cabinet flew to San Luis, where he organized the press conference announcing his resignation.

But San Luis was seven hundred miles from Buenos Aires, and we needed his written resignation in Congress in order to appoint his successor. It was the first ever resignation sent by fax. Amazing. I began negotiating his succession with Ramon Puerta, the president of the Senate, who was by law Rodriguez Saá's successor. But Puerta did not want the burden of the role and suggested the president of the Chamber of Deputies, Caamaño. I mentioned to Puerta that if Caamaño didn't accept it, I would offer the position to the president of the Supreme Court, the next in line, who had been appointed by Menem with no merit but that he was formerly Menem's partner in law. That would be unthinkable for Duhalde, who was behind the whole event. Caamaño finally accepted.

But, with the resignation of Rodriguez Saá, another problem emerged. Rodriguez Saá was being indicted for abandoning his mandate, a crime under Argentine law. I held my final meeting as Secretary of Justice with the federal judge in charge, explaining that Rodriguez Saá was legally in office until the new president was installed by vote of Congress.

Rodriguez Saa TV resignation

I remained in office until January 3, 2002, when the new Secretary of Justice, appointed by Eduardo Duhalde, the new provisional President, took my place. Then, it was over. Amazing.

I hadn't the time to consider the enormity of what had just occurred.

In January, the courts were in recess. In February, I would resume my position as private prosecutor in the AMIA trial, and life, I hoped, would return to normal. Easily said—but life in Argentina was not easy. I began to wonder whether this was the future I wished for my family.

12

THE JUDGMENT

In January 2002, my wife and I took our two small children on our first holiday to a coastal resort not far from Buenos Aires. The previous January, I had been working in Washington, preparing our statement to the ICHR. I hadn't realized my own state of mind after the events of the past year. I had never been a great fan of holidays, but being a father totally changed my perspective. For a few days, it was just us and the immense Atlantic Ocean, the marveled expression of our three-year-old son as the waves broke on the sand, leaving flecks of foam and bits of shell, and the welcome slumber of our two-month-old daughter. I slept long hours, lulled by the sea, and I felt myself reinvigorated. The pleasure of being awakened by one's children, their laughter and tears, feeding them, caressing them, just being there—it was a wonderful sensation I discovered with fresh eyes.

It was strange to be seated again in my former place when the sessions resumed in February. Stranger still was the aspect of the audience hall. Now, the public occupied only a few seats, and a lone pair of reporters covered the trial. Little seemed to have happened with the case, and public interest had steadily waned.

One by one, the long list of witnesses spoke before the court.

It was time for members of the fire department to speak. They described the collection of evidence from the site of the explosion, which had been done without following procedural formalities; even the corpses and human remains were collected without precaution, all gathered together in a single bag. The case was a mess. We knew it already, but the fact was now reaching the public. It was discovered, for instance, that the report on the engine's discovery was falsified.

Originally, a member of the security forces had declared that the motor was found within the shovel of a bulldozer clearing the site. Before the court, however, he claimed the motor was discovered first by the members of the Israeli army who had come to assist in the clean-up, and produced several photographs taken within the Israelis' tent, showing the soldiers together with the engine.

Israeli rescuers group working at the AMIA site

That was a problem. If the original report of the engine's discovery had been falsified, the defense might plant some doubt as to whether the engine even belonged to the attackers' van. The court could always refer to the tribunal's chemical analysis of the engine, proving that it had in fact survived such temperatures as would be reached in an explosion. However, such an analysis had not been performed during the instruction time, and this decision of the oral tribunal affirmed our claim that there had never been a proper search for evidence.

Doctors from the morgue and the SAME, the state-run emergency medical institution usually called to assist in case of catastrophes, as well as members of the police force and the fire department, all of whom had assisted in the aftermath of the explosion, described their efforts.

Several residents of Pasteur Street confirmed the presence of a helicopter the night before the blast. In response, two air controllers explained the police's need for a helicopter that night, due to the crowd that had gathered in celebration of Brazil's victory at the World Cup. However, that crowd had gathered in the vicinity of the Brazilian Embassy, several kilometers from the AMIA building, in another quarter of Buenos Aires, nowhere near the AMIA building where the helicopter seemed to be searching. All these witnesses had been called to give testimony for the first time, once again suggesting the clumsiness of Galeano's investigation.

Between the end of May and the beginning of June, we heard the testimonies of the people who had been in charge of Jet-Parking, where the van was presumably parked until July 16. Proprietors of vehicles parked in the same lot were called for the first time, though they revealed nothing new. Yet the person in charge of a closed lot across the street from Jet-Parking gave a very important testimony. This man, who previously worked in the Air Force, related with great accuracy how the driver of the van, speaking broken Spanish with a heavy foreign accent, tried to convince him to park the van on the upper floor of his lot. The problem, the parking man explained, was that the van was too tall to pass through the roof of the ramp in the upper floor. The entire conversation, several minutes long, was captured on his security cameras. After the explosion, this person said, he contacted the security forces; people from the Federal Police appeared at the parking lot, to whom he described the incident and revealed the existence of the videotape. The agents informed him that he would be called to testify, and that he should bring the tape with him. But he never heard from them again, and, after two years, the tape was reused.

We were astonished at his testimony. On the one hand, we couldn't understand why this evidence had not been collected immediately, nor why Galeano had not later determined what measures to take concerning the collection of such fundamental evidence. It was easy, as often happened in the AMIA case, to attribute such missteps to the incompetence of Galeano and the security forces. But to allow the loss of such evidence suggested a disregard beyond simple clumsiness. We began to wonder about the content of that tape. Did it show the SIDE agents who had infiltrated the group? If so, we can assume it would not be difficult at all for SIDE to obtain the tape by other means. Why did the man in charge of the parking lot not take special care of the tape, having realized its content? In any case, beyond all possible speculation, it proved once again the poverty of the investigation into the most important terrorist attack carried out within Argentina. That was an essential aspect of our complaint to the ICHR, and we were being proven doubtlessly correct.

Months passed without many breakthroughs. In August, a group of professors from Louisiana State University arrived for a summer course in Buenos Aires, and, considering I might seek a professorship in the United States, I provided one of them a copy of my CV. I had a personal contact with Saul Litvinoff, a Boyd Professor living since 1970 in Baton Rouge, and he belonged to the group. Perhaps raising my family in the U.S. was preferable to a country where so much of daily life was confused and uncertain, where the systems of justice seemed only to obstruct the truth; where presidents resigned by television, and one is threatened for bringing justice to murderers. Now my wife and I had two young children, and I wondered whether this was the life I wished for them.

As tends to happen when confronting one's destiny, some doors opened while others swung shut. Sometimes, electing the correct path is a complicated matter; other times it is smooth and easy. More than anything, I wanted to escape the public exposure and political dealings which, of late, had dominated my life.

In October, I received a call from the Dean of the Law Faculty at Louisiana State University, inviting me to give a conference in Baton Rouge. I returned to that place where I had been once before, in 1987. As it happened in Via Rasella in Rome, so it happened in Baton Rouge; such coincidences always make me wonder. It was hot and humid, as Louisiana always seems to be. My presentation went smoothly, and the university staff seemed friendly and welcoming. Every day I ate lunch and dinner with a different group of people, and took part of my last day to film a bit of Baton Rouge, to show at home. After all, this would not be my decision alone.

A week after my return, I received a formal offer from the Dean for the position of law professor at LSU. I discussed the matter with my family, and we decided to accept. It was not an easy decision, but the United States offered the future we desired, without so much turmoil. The AMIA trial was ending, and the investigation would not continue for a long while. We had proved the authenticity of our complaint not only to the tribunal, but to the ICHR as well. Anyway, my colleagues and I would be in touch. By 2003, communications had changed; we were connected across the globe; I would be able to assist Pablo in everything he required. He would take care of the final plea, and I would read the judgment in Baton Rouge.

Baton Rouge seemed to me a lovely provincial city. I felt the immediate charm of the place, which I hoped would convince my wife that we had made the right decision. We found a nice home in a semi-private residential quarter near the university, and returned to Buenos Aires to prepare for our move. The time to say our goodbye had come. I bid farewell to the judges of the TOF, to my colleagues from Defense and Prosecution, and I was ready to go. I flew to the United States three months in advance of my family, in order to prepare the house, make some changes, and receive the delivery of our furniture from Buenos Aires.

Louisiana had many advantages for an attorney rooted in the civil law tradition. First of all, Louisiana is proud to be the only State that retains a Civil Code, a product of its French and Spanish history. I would discover that things were not as I had anticipated, that, as a matter of fact, the influence of the Common Law is very strong. It would be fair to talk about a mixed jurisdiction better than a civil one. But everything was new to me. A trip to near New Orleans would re-introduce me to the delight of American jazz and the French Quarter. The glorious smells of magnolias in summer. In Buenos Aires, I had spotted the few that marked my daily jogging of three miles, but in Louisiana they were everywhere, even in my own garden I had two magnolia trees.

Louisiana State University had a fantastic campus. I was surprised to see the size of the football stadium, at least two times the size of the largest soccer stadium in Argentina. The library of the Law Faculty, too, was huge, very well provisioned and open 24 hours. We were provided all the requisite tools for our research. The Paul M. Hebert Law Center where I worked took its name from a former dean, who had served as a justice in the Nuremberg trials. All his archives were there, and I was engaged once again with World War II.

Paul M. Hebert Law Center at Louisiana State University in Baton Rouge

My family arrived in October 2003. The house was ready to receive them. It was very comfortable, each child had a bedroom, and I installed all the eight huge bookshelves with my books. My time in the United States was not going to be happy, though I didn't know it then. My wife suffered most of all because she did not understand English properly, and was soon immersed in a depression from which she took several months to recover. It was not easy, both taking care of the children and attending to my work as a professor. I was stressed in a way I had never experienced before.

Pablo in the meantime began to prepare our final statement for the AMIA case. Most of the work had been done already. Our claim to the ICHR was fully proved.

The last session of the tribunal took place on December 29, 2003. On January 12, the parties began to read their final pleas. The process took more than ten days. Memoria Activa only accused Telleldin as an accomplice. By 2004, he had been imprisoned nearly eight years, and apparently preferred his confinement to the risk of confession. It was clear to everybody that Telleldin at least knew the true recipient of the van. Nonetheless, attributing to him a more important role in the bombing would have been mere speculation. Nothing suggested he had connections to the terrorist group, much less with the planning, execution, and cover-up of the attack. Technically his crime was concealment, the punishment for which was upwards of six years in prison. We accused him of participation in the bombing, which heightened the severity of his crime, allowing us to keep him in prison a while longer.

After the trial, however, we were no longer in a position to accuse him of anything but concealment, and the time he had spent in prison so far meant the TOF could release him. Anyway, our main objective had been reached. We had shown beyond all doubt that the investigation hardly existed in any meaningful form, and that Galeano and Menem had willfully concealed many important pieces of evidence; all their work was legally null. Pablo presented our plea, pointing out that the case had proven a massive violation of human rights, multiplied by the concealment by the Argentine state. He stated that after the trial, we knew exactly what we knew in the first days following the attack—not because of the TOF 3, but due to the remarkable attitude of the judge in charge of the investigation. The collection of evidence was marked by clumsiness, and beyond criminal negligence had shown the clear inability of the Argentine security forces to handle an event of such magnitude. Pablo said it was inconceivable that the investigators had never even called the first responders to give testimony. He claimed that the accusation against the police officers was spurious, without basis, made only after Telleldin had reached an agreement with Galeano. The Argentine state had failed in its duty to sufficiently investigate the attack, as the Inter-American Commission on Human Rights mandates, and such a failure deserved condemnation. Pablo criticized Galeano's behavior in performing a parallel investigation, without control and including procedural institutions not defined within Argentine law. All this lacked any objective but to construct a facade, a cover-up that had been exposed by the end of the trial.

On September 2, 2004, after two and half years of trial, the tribunal president read the judgment, the complete details of which, expounded in more than four thousand pages, would be given to the parties and the public twenty days later. It was clear that the members of the TOF 3 had been gathering documents in advance of their decision, in order to prepare that lengthy declaration. Thus they ended the sessions with a more or less completed statement, resulting from a reasoned and considerate evaluation of the evidence. They considered all the circumstances of Galeano's investigation, and finally ordered the indictment of Galeano along with the public prosecutors Muellen and Barbaccia, under such crimes as the falsification and destruction of evidence, abuse of power, deprivation of freedom, and concealment.

On February 22, 2005, Dean Claudio Grossman produced his report, which can be read today on the internet. It demolished the official version of the AMIA case, underscoring everything proven during the trial, and recommended our claim be accepted at the ICHR.

On March 4, I flew from Baton Rouge to Washington, D.C. It was a sunny day, cold still, but admitting a hint of the coming spring. I arrived at the Pan American Union Building, headquarters for the Organization of American States, on 17th Street and Constitution Avenue. An impressive structure, with

Meeting at the OAS in Washington

white stone steps arriving at the elegant marble façade, including, on either side of the entryway, two friezes representing North and South America. Three magnificent bronze gates lead to a Spanish patio with a tropical garden, palms and rare plants blooming all year round, lightened beneath a clear glass roof. Built at the beginning of the twentieth century, this elegant mansion is otherwise known as the House of the Americas. Within the hall, Pablo, Diana, and Adriana—President of Memoria Activa following Norma's death—awaited me. We greeted each other, like soldiers reunited after battle. We had proved our complaint, and were gathered at the OAS Building for the grand finale.

We met the representatives of the ICHR and the Argentine government in a small office in the first floor, where, lacking sufficient seating, I stood in the corner, looking onto the scene. Méndez Carreras, the representative of the Argentine government, expressed his desire to

The OAS building in Washington where the meeting took place

make a statement. He stood, took a sip of water, and began to read: "*The Argentine government recognizes the state's responsibility for the violation of human rights claimed by Memoria Activa, including the right to life, to physical integrity and to judicial protection. The state recognizes its responsibility, because there was no prevention to avoid the attack; the state acknowledges its responsibility, because there was a cover-up and a denial of justice.*" I felt a lump in my throat and could hardly contain my tears. Such words, unthinkable at the beginning of our struggle, were now being pronounced by the representative of my own country, surely having been prepared together with the Argentine authorities. I think our group was prepared to negotiate an arrangement with Argentina, but we never expected a total surrender. It was beyond our most optimistic expectations. It was not only a formal surrender, but a confession and acceptance of guilt.

These words concluded the imbalanced struggle between the state and ourselves, a small group of people, trying to win their right to justice. Hearing those words, I admit, left me emotionally drained. I had fought with all my power, first alone and then with Pablo, against the President, against Galeano, against the public prosecutors, the secret services, the security forces, even against some Jewish institutions. It was a balm to hear their recognition of guilt, justifying all the sacrifices we had made. Our small group gathered in the Hall of the Americas, and among the marble columns and the statues of American heroes, we embraced. Our war had ended. We had not achieved our main objective, to indict the local connection to the bombing; but we had proved beyond all doubt that the judge and the government had impeded the investigation in a way that rendered true justice impossible. It was a victory, by all means, but a bitter one.

That night, returning to Baton Rouge, I walked in peace through my home, looked in on my sleeping wife and children, and sat down to begin work on the first pages of this book.

EPILOGUE

Following my departure from Argentina and the AMIA case—which had hardly progressed at all by the time I returned in 2009—a couple of events should be mentioned.

TOF 3's decision not only confirmed our expectations about the concealment and the acquittal of the people prosecuted by Galeano; it also required the investigation in a separate proceeding of all those functionaries implicated in the concealment. Thirteen people were indicted, in addition to Galeano and the prosecutors Muelen and Barbaccia: former president Menem, former Secretary of State Corach, and the former president of DAIA, Ruben Beraja; Hugo Anzorregui, the director of the SIDE, and his undersecretary, Juan Carlos Anchezar; Patricio Finnen, director of the so-called Sala Patria of the SIDE, who worked closely with Galeano; Fino Palacios, chief of the Antiterrorist section of the Federal Police; Carlos Castaneda, chief of the unit Protection of Constitutional Order (POC) of the Federal Police, who signed page 114; Telleldin, accused of embezzlement for the US $400,000 transactions, his wife, Ana Boragni, and his lawyer, Victor Stinfale, all for the same operation. Finally, the people who were reponsible for the the concealment were going to be prosecuted. That was an additional triumph.

TOF 2 took charge of the prosecution of those deemed complicit in the cover-up, and audiences began on August 8, 2015. The private prosecutors for the case were Memoria Activa, now represented by other counselors; AMIA, DAIA; Apemia, the new organization founded by Laura Ginsberg; and the group of policemen indicted in the first AMIA trial. The official prosecution was in charge of two accusers, appointed by the AMIA Unit directed by Nisman. Menem, Galeano, Castañeda, Stinfale and Anzorreguy refused to testify. The SIDE members testified in private, without public witness.

The policemen declared their unjust imprisonment by Galeano, while Diana Malamud and Adriana Rosenfel testified about the obstructions to our investigation. I had been proposed as a witness for the prosecutors, but my testimony was opposed by Galeano, Muellen and Barbaccia.

After more than three years of audiences, at the end of 2017 began the final pleadings of the parties. Surprisingly, the Minister of Justice ordered that the former prosecutors Muellen and Barbaccia should not be accussed. That was origin of another scandal, because it was presumed that the reason for such astonishing behavior from the official prosecution was the friendship that the current Minister of Justice Garavano hold with Muellen and Barbaccia. On the contrary, Memoria Activa during its pleading requested 20 years of prison for Galeano, 13 years for Muellen and Barbaccia, 6 years of prison for former president Menem, and 10 years for the former director of the SIDE Anzorreguy, among others. A final decision could be expected at the end of 2018.

The second point that I would like to mention is related, as I've said, to the origin of the terrorist attack, which according to the official version propounded by Galeano, had always been Iran. Yet, until 2003, no one had been charged with the attack. President Néstor Kirchner, who assumed office that year, called this failure of the AMIA investigation a national disgrace, and, with the consent of AMIA, DAIA, and even Memoria Activa, appointed Alberto Nisman as special prosecutor to the case. That was, in my opinion, a terrible mistake: they had granted greater power to somebody who would only continue Galeano's own methods. I was indignant that Pablo had consented to Nisman's appointment. But Pablo was Jewish, as was Nisman, and he was better prepared than I to change his opinion of Nisman.

Nisman in his office as special prosecutor for the AMIA investigation

In 2006, Nisman charged Hezbollah with the bombing of the AMIA building, and later produced a list of six Iranian officers and diplomats connected with the attack. Among the indicted was former Iranian President Ali Akbar Hashemi Rafsanjani. In the case of the indictment of such a high-ranking government official, an investigation into his possible immunity was required. The matter is complex, but in international law the subject had been resolved with a treaty and some jurisprudence: first, the 1961 Vienna Convention on Diplomatic Relations; then, a case in 2000 decided by the International Court of Justice. These materials elaborate upon the terms of immunity for a governmental official during his time in office, and dictate when and how this immunity might be invalidated. However, unless something very important occurred during my absence, Nisman's indictment was going to be exceedingly difficult to prove. Nonetheless, a federal judge issued international arrest warrants for several of these men.

On March 15, 2007, Interpol's Executive Committee approved the so-called "Red Notices" issued to six of the accused, among them Foreign Minister Velayati and Ambassador Soleimanpour, who was in charge of the Iranian Embassy in Buenos Aires at the time of the bombing—not including, however, President Rafsanjani. Evidence shows that the United States assisted Nisman in seeking the issuance of the Red Notices from Interpol; the U.S. Embassy in Argentina and the Office of International Affairs in the U.S. Department of Justice even helped Nisman to craft his request. This is true—keeping in mind Nisman's several visits to Washington, D.C., his public request of support from the United States, and his exchange with Washington, later released by WikiLeaks.

On September 26, 2007, in his last address to the United Nations General Assembly, President Néstor Kirchner denounced Iran's failure to cooperate in the investigation, and urged the UN member states to support the extradition of the accused Iranian officials. His wife, Cristina Fernández de

Néstor Kirschner addressing the United Nations General Assembly

Kirchner, who would assume the presidency in December 2007, brought about an unexpected change with regard to this policy.

One thing should be emphasized: as I had predicted, Nisman was merely an extension of Galeano; under his charge, the case did not move an inch. He benefitted just as Galeano had before him: he was provided total independence, an inexhaustible revenue, and many valuable resources to dispose of as he saw fit. Nor did Nisman produce any valuable evidence or obtain any information regarding the terrorists' local connection. It was easier to focus on the international plots, difficult to prove and wasteful of time, while Nisman was paid regardless.

Soon after his assignment, Nisman divorced from his wife, a federal judge named Arroyo Salgado, and was often seen at Buenos Aires' many night clubs, with any one of his various girlfriends.

However, events would soon arise to undermine Nisman's tranquility: in January 2013, after several months of secret negotiations, Argentina signed the aptly titled "Memorandum of Understanding between the Government of Argentina and the Government of the Islamic Republic of Iran on the issues related to the terrorist attack against AMIA headquarter in Buenos Aires on July 18, 1994."

Photo of the signature of the Memorandum of Understanding between Argentina and Iran. In the photo sign former Argentine Foreign Minister Timerman and Iranian Foreign Minister Salehi.

The memorandum established a so-called "truth commission" of international lawyers, not one among them a citizen of Argentina or Iran, to analyze the documentation presented by the judicial authorities of either country. The commissioners would review the evidence and conduct an investigation of each accused individual; then, they would provide their recommendation. *"Both parties will take into account these recommendations in their future actions."* In a separate article entitled "Hearings," it was stated: *"The Commission, the Argentine and Iranian judicial authorities will meet in Tehran to proceed to questioning of whom Interpol has issued a red notice. The Commission will have authority to pose questions to the representatives of either side, [and] each side has the right to give explanations or submit new documents during the meetings."* A specific article stated that when the agreement was signed, both Chancelleries would send a copy to the Secretary General of Interpol, *"as a fulfillment of Interpol's requirements regarding this case."*

This Memorandum of Understanding would be in effect once approved by the relevant bodies of each country.

Such a work perfectly reflected the missteps typical of the AMIA case. First, President Kirchner had appealed to the UN member states to aid Argentina in its pursuit of information from Iran; and now, suddenly, this dubious agreement arose after several months of negotiations, which was not mandatory and in fact allowed Iran to deny any possible liability. Even the article stating that a copy would be sent to Interpol was not clear, so that they did not have to rescind the Red Notices. It was another cruel joke.

At the time, Argentina was badly in need of oil, and Iran was the perfect place to find it. The Kirchner administration had approached Venezuela, then under the rule of Hugo Chávez, who was in turn contacted by the Iranian government, seeking help in improving relations with Argentina. In this context, the Chancelleries of Iran and Argentina began work on what became the Memorandum of Understanding. One might conceive that, in order to obtain the signature of this document, the Iranian had bribed the Kirchner administration. Whatever the reasons that inspired the Argentine Chancellery to sign this abomination, one thing was clear: Nisman's position was no longer secure, and, without saying so explicitly, the Memorandum attacked all the work he had done so far (what little that might have been).

Several nongovernmental organizations, together with members of the Jewish communities, human rights groups, and jurists of various origin, protested vehemently against the Memorandum. Not only because it provided no assurance that an impartial investigation would be conducted, but also because it violated the governmental division of powers; the only party to benefit would be Iran.

Nisman was enraged. He appealed to the judge appointed to replace Galeano, insisting upon the unconstitutionality of the Memorandum of Understanding, explaining that the Executive branch cannot nullify judicial functions. Clearly such an appeal earned him Kirchner's close attention. His position as Special Prosecutor was questioned. Nisman's shortsightedness blinded him to changes in the political sphere: the government no longer belonged to Néstor Kirchner, who, until his death in 2010, had been Nisman's main supporter. Cristina, with her court of sycophants, was determined to become the reincarnation of Eva Perón; she stamped her presidency with a demagogic stance against imperialism. The Chávez government in Venezuela, which had financed a part of her campaign, was perfect for these purposes, and Chávez's strong links to Iran provided the latter a means to mend its difficulties with Argentina.

In Buenos Aires, the debate over the constitutionality of the Memorandum occurred at all levels. Jewish institutions rejected the document, along with the many jurists who expressed their opinions in the media. Yet, having the majority in both Chambers of the Congress, the Memorandum was approved on February 27, 2013. Iran, however, perhaps due to the intricacy and obscurity of the text, failed to formally approve the Memorandum. In May 2014, the main Jewish institutions appealed to the Chamber of Appeals, and the Memorandum was declared unconstitutional.

Nisman, meanwhile, took a grave risk. In January 2015, he returned abruptly from his holidays in Europe to announce a claim of treason against President Cristina Kirchner. Evidently, he had been preparing his indictment before his departure. He accused Kirchner of plotting to provide immunity to the Iranian officials, who, according to him, had been involved with the AMIA bombing. He spoke of aggravated concealment and a violation of the duties of a public official, perpetrated by President Kirchner and Foreign Minister Héctor Timerman, among other lateral functionaries within the administration.

Opinion was divided across the country, between those who pondered with incredulity Nisman's statement and those who dismissed the claim as unfounded speculation. On Friday,

January 16, 2015, Nisman gave an interview on television, which I had the chance to attend. He spoke more quickly than usual, explaining that he possessed solid evidence that Kirchner and the Ministry of Foreign Affairs favored the Memorandum for purely financial reasons. He was to appear at Congress the following Monday, where a severe interrogation was anticipated.

At the TV political show "A dos voces" Nisman, in what was going to be his last interview, indicted president Cristina Kirschner

That weekend, I read Nisman's two-hundred-and-ninety-page manuscript, available then on the internet. After a lengthy introduction, he began to describe the evidence that would sustain his accusation, insisting upon his proof with such repeated proclamations as, "*it will be proved by multiple pieces of evidence,*" or "*this will be shown clearly from the evidence presented,*" and so on. In one instance, he claimed that this evidence was only "the tip of the iceberg," and that many of the stated accusations had been performed "acting personally," rather than as governmental officials. Finally, he explained that most of his evidence consisted of transcriptions of telephone conversations between the government functionaries aforementioned and journalists from various newspapers.

The indictment was a fiasco. What manner of evidence could be discovered in a labor leader's conversation with a member of the Chamber of Deputies, mentioning an order "from upstairs"? How could a jurist consider such private conversations sufficient evidence? After one hundred and twenty pages, I was certain a scandal was approaching, which would only benefit the government. Despite my desire to discover some manner of evidence implicating Cristina Kirchner, I was yet astonished that Nisman had been so enthralled with mere hearsay. He would be destroyed before Congress, embarrassed in a way I never anticipated; and despite the fact that I wished him to prove something, accusations based on such miserable evidence only proved me correct: Nisman was at least candid. I cannot say I thought him an enemy, but I had no pity for him. He had participated in Galeano's plot, and the other prosecutors certainly wanted him gone. But he had been the least complicit among them, and I would have been satisfied with his mere removal from the case. More than anything, he was a clear participant in those events. That weekend seemed to consist only of discussions of Nisman's accusations. Of course, the media being dominated mostly by the official party, everyone was against him. *"We are going to go with bared teeth,"* said a deputy of the official party.

Then, on Sunday, January 18, Nisman was found dead, with a bullet in his skull.

The country was in shock. Friends called from abroad, asking my opinion. Nobody was sure what had happened. I considered for a moment that, having thrown out his career on a conjecture, Nisman suddenly realized that he was going to be destroyed before the public, and so he killed himself. But, after a while, I thought that was a naïve conclusion. Nisman didn't seem the depressive type, and he had even spoken with a national deputy hours before; he was in high spirits. Moreover, anybody who had read his statement would have realized that it contained nothing substantial, and that no court of law would uphold such conjecture and hearsay. Yet it was conceivable that somebody in the government or otherwise mentioned in Nisman's statement had determined to end his life, without inquiring further into his claims.

Nisman lived in a very expensive apartment in one of the most exclusive quarters of Buenos Aires. The building included twenty-four-hour surveillance, with security guards and a camera system—but, when investigators looked into it, the system was found not to be functioning. At least, that was what the media was informed. The first photographs of the scene at the building began to appear on TV. A member of the Executive branch had been there from the first moment, even before the judge or the prosecutor. The most dramatic of the images was the crowd of police officers, firemen, security forces, and members of the judiciary, trampling into Nisman's apartment. Again, we were witness to the destruction of evidence and the contamination of a crime scene. It was tragic irony that this should occur with Nisman's death: he had collaborated with Galeano before, to make a similar mess of the AMIA case. Now, life—or death —had determined it was his turn.

A crowd of policemen, firemen and investigators with the prosecutor (the woman in the first row) at Nisman apartment (photo from the Federal Police)

According to the initial reports, Nisman's mother was called by his security guards because he was not answering their ringing at the apartment, nor their several phone calls. His mother, first having tried to reach him by phone, and later arriving to find the door to his apartment locked, finally called a locksmith. They entered, along with the security guard, the National Security Secretary Berni, and the Chief of the Federal Police, and discovered him where he lay: in his bathroom, in a pool of his own blood, wearing shorts and a T-shirt, with a bullet hole in his head. A .22 caliber pistol was found beneath his body. Images of the intervening prose-

The bathroom where Nisman was found. The prosecutor Fein stepping in one blood spot (photo Argentine Federal Police). The used pistol was placed at the sink by the investigators

cutor at the site, stepping through the blood beside a policeman, proved once again the clumsiness of investigators.

At first, there was some confusion, State Security Secretary Berni presuming that Nisman might be merely hurt, and they called a private medical doctor. When this man arrived, he confirmed that Nisman had been dead for several hours.

The gun, it was later confirmed, belonged to an assistant of Nisman's, a Mr. Lagomarsino, who told authorities that Nisman had called him to the apartment on Saturday morning and, when he arrived, requested the gun. Lagomarsino then returned to his home in San Isidro, more than twenty miles from Nisman's apartment, picked up the pistol, and immediately delivered it. The story was somehow difficult to believe. That Nisman—who, it turned out, already owned several guns—would not mention the pistol until his assistant had arrived at the apartment—knowing that Lagomarsino had just driven the twenty miles from his own home—was remarkable. Why would Nisman ask for a gun of such small caliber? Why didn't he ask for the gun on the telephone, if that was the purpose of his call? Why did Lagomarsino not wonder at Nisman's request?

Mr. Lagomarsino who owned the pistol used in Nisman fatal gunshot

A paraffin test to detect traces of powder on Nisman's hands was unsuccessful. A more complex test, conducted after some delay, finally proved that his hands bore no trace of having handle a gun. Nisman's autopsy revealed that his body had been moved from its original position, as traces of blood were found on one of his arms. Blood was found in the sink, too, as though someone had washed his or her blood there.

Kirchner's government upheld the claim of suicide, as did the acting prosecutor. Nobody could have expected any different.

Nisman's family, on the contrary, declared that Nisman had been murdered. The government began a smear campaign against Nisman. Suddenly, he was presented to Argentine society in several private photos with young girls, vacationing in Mexico, or dancing in a disco.

Finally, an undeclared bank account containing more than US $700,000 was discovered in the United States, with Nisman, his mother, and Lagomarsino listed as the account managers. Apart from tax avoidance, the purpose of the account was unclear. Later, it was also revealed that Nisman and Lagomarsino had traveled together to Chile, presumably with the idea of buying clothes. Everything looked very strange. Had somebody checked Lagomarsino's attire when he entered Nisman's apartment? And when he departed? Had anybody studied the surveillance tapes for the quarter where Nisman lived? Presumably, the person who shot him was near his body when the shot occurred, and the blood stains on the wall of the bathroom showed splatters and spots of blood that would very likely have flecked anyone who was there. Had somebody checked whether clothes were lacking from Nisman's wardrobe. Why was the State Security Secretary at the apartment before the judge or even the police? The gun showed no evidence of having been passed to Nisman, no DNA or fingerprints. However, as seen in the films presented on television, several people were at the apartment, and the gun was carelessly handled, there even being a photo of somebody holding the gun full of blood, though with surgical gloves.

Nisman had once again divided the population, now between those who believed he had committed suicide, and those who believed he had been murdered. Among the latter was a further division, between those who believed in a government conspiracy and those who accused Lagomarsino. The evidence didn't resolve the question. Some claimed the autopsy had proved Nisman's suicide, because a lesion on one of his hands suggested the slide had recoiled and cut him. Others claimed that the entry wound, a few inches above and behind the left ear, as well as the projectile trajectory, required a manner of handling the weapon incompatible with suicide; that the shooting hand was clean because another hand had been covering it from behind, and that he had received the lesion in self-defense. The initial autopsy, performed without the permission of the private prosecution for Nisman's daughters, determined that it was a suicide. The private prosecutors, however, later prepared a report based on a film of the autopsy, and arrived to the opposite conclusion. They disagreed even over Nisman's time of death.

The Nisman case remains open as I write these pages—as does the AMIA bombing. However, it was clear that police protocol in the collection of evidence had not been followed in either case. Evidence of the bombing sits forever at the bottom of the Río de la Plata. Nisman's case, on the other hand, is too fresh to be drowned.

When, in 2005, the Argentine government accepted with full responsibility our claim to the ICHR, it was obliged to perform several measures: to indemnify the victims of the AMIA bombing, and to install a forensic unit provided with the latest scientific developments to collect evidence, in case a similar event should happen again. When a proper search for evidence has been done with regard to Nisman, we will surely discover more about his murder than we know today.

A federal judge who analyzed Nisman's indictment against Kirchner decided to archive it without further consideration. I agree that the indictment was unfounded, but that was not the correct approach. The indictment deserved some investigation, at the least. If nothing could be corroborated, then closing the case would have been legally correct. But its abrupt dismissal helped nothing. Everybody was suddenly convinced that something very wrong was being hidden. Sudden protests arose; a march was organized to demand a transparent investigation of Nisman's death. Nisman's tragic demise had transformed him into an icon of the victimized. Ironically, his protection of the clumsy and corrupt procedural system during the AMIA investigation today prevents us from discovering the truth of his death.

In December 2015, a new administration was elected, with Mauricio Macri assuming the presidency. Now, for the first time in nearly 100 years, the government is neither Peronist nor Radical. It has not been easy, but it seems we as a nation are finally moving towards normalcy. The new Argentine government has encouraged a full investigation of the AMIA case. The decision to close Nisman's indictment has been revoked, and that case, too, has been reopened. The TOF 2 trial continues as I write these lines; perhaps a decision will be made by the end of 2018. I can only hope the refreshing breezes now passing across the surface of Argentina will someday uncover some of the mysteries that remain hidden beneath. Perhaps we will soon have some justice.

The AMIA building today at Pasteur 633. The first names of all the victims are written in white

AFTERWORD

I hope that you have enjoyed "AMIA - An Ongoing Crime", and that it has shed new light on the worst terrorist act to occur on Argentinian soil.

If you enjoyed this book, please consider leaving a review on Amazon by clicking on the link below so that other interested readers can learn more about this devastating act against the AMIA in Buenos Aires in 1994.

http://bit.ly/AMIA-Zuppi

Thank You!

ACKNOWLEDGMENTS

I would like to thank Ronnie Stutes and Jasper Miller Patterson for their fine suggestions, to my dear Elsa Tracchia who helped me with the first draft of this book, that sadly coudn't make it to see it published, and to my friends Enrique Ahumada and Cesar Chelala for their encouragement.

And with great thanks for the cover photo from a newspaper in Buenos Aires, along with other photos throughout the book, which belong to the Telam Agency.

ABOUT THE AUTHOR

Alberto Luis Zuppi is Argentine attorney, author of several books and scholarly articles on different aspects of international criminal law, Zuppi also served as Robert and Pamela Martin Professor at the Paul M. Herbert Law Center of Louisiana State University. He holds a PhD (Magna cum laude) from Saarland University, Germany.

Alberto Luis Zuppi (Photo by Viktor Ems)

www.ingramcontent.com/pod-product-compliance
Lightning Source LLC
Chambersburg PA
CBHW030112100526
44591CB00009B/380